D1367525

UNDERSTANDING ABORIGINAL CULTURE

Front Cover: The large figure in the centre is the Wirinun making a psychic link with the spirit ancestors in order to obtain advice and healing energies for the purpose of healing the patient depicted by the smaller figure inside the Wirinun. Tya and its inhabitants are surrounded by an invisible sheath which is only broken by intense spiritual power from the Dowie dimension. Assistance comes to the Wirinun from spirit ancestor healers, totemic spirits, the sun, stars and other supernatural beings.

Note the energy streaming through the top of the head, the result of deep mental concentration by the Wirinun. The energy flows through the fingers to the affected part of the patient's body.

UNDERSTANDING ABORIGINAL CULTURE

CYRIL HAVECKER

Illustrations
CYRIL HAVECKER

Edited and Foreword by
Yvonne Malykke

COSMOS

Published by
Cosmos Periodicals
PO Box 626 Murwillumbah NSW
Australia 2484

Reprinted 1988, 1991, 1994, 1996, 1999

National Library of Australia card number
and ISBN 0 9588588 0 2

Designed by Yvonne Malykke

Printed in Australia by McPherson's Printing Group

CONTENTS

FOREWORD

It was the desire to preserve a cultural heritage which prompted me to ask Cyril Havecker to write about Aboriginal culture.

We met in 1972 and as both of us had a deep interest in metaphysics there was a common bond. We remained good friends until his death on April 18th, 1979.

In 1973 I co-founded the successful and controversial national monthly New Age counter-culture journal **Cosmos**. The first issue was published in June, 1973. One year later I became Editor and remained so until its closing in July, 1983. During those ten years **Cosmos** readership extended to eighteen countries. The story of this unique publication is recorded in the book *In Pursuit of the Spiritual Cosmos.*

It was 1974 when I approached Cyril Havecker for a series of articles on Aboriginal culture and in January, 1976 published the first of the series. They were published again in 1982. I also sponsored for him a series of lectures and workshops in 1978 where members met to discuss the myths and legends of the Aborigines who were the shamans of Australia. These workshops were attended by a number of young Aborigines interested to learn, for the first time, something of their culture.

Cyril believed that the Aborigines were in Australia when the pyramids were being built in Egypt and that Australia was originally populated by highly intelligent beings ~ now the Dreamtime heroes of Aboriginal mythology. The universe, he said, was created as the result of a dream, intense desire, emotion and directed thought by Baiame. He spoke of the physical manifestation of this great spirit at Lake Narran some 10,000 years ago.

Aborigines still revere Lake Narran (near Brewarrina, NSW) and surrounding lands, claiming it to be a high energy centre.

The belief in the Laws of the Dreamtime brought down by the Supreme Intelligence, Creator or Baiame are shared by all initiated Aborigines, regardless of the tribe to which they belong

When the first white settlers arrived in Australia there were approximately seven hundred dialects derived from two hundred separate languages, each tribe possessing its own cultural distinction. The name of the Creator alters in different regions to Bunjil, Join, Nurunderi and so on, but without exception it was this first intelligence that gave the Aborigines their social and religious laws and instituted the initiation rites.

The secret initiation grounds known as the Bora ring supposedly represent the body of the Supreme Being or the universe, of which every living thing, yowie or soul is a part. Traditional Aboriginal life and law is pervaded by religious consciousness. They live by the Laws of the Dreamtime.

Cyril Havecker was born in the small town of Murray Plains, South Australia, now a ghost town. There were twenty-four children at the public school of which eighteen were Aborigines and Cyril would spend his leisure time visiting their camps and listening to their stories.

His father kept horses and was a friend of the champion buck jumper of Australia, John Kardell, who was an initiated Aborigine from the Arunta tribe. It was John who first taught Cyril so much about Aboriginal culture and took him to many of the caves to explain the esoteric significance of the paintings.

Later Cyril went to Groote Eylandt and lived close to the Warramunga Tribe, becoming a blood brother.

We had many long and interesting discussions on the metaphysical aspects of the culture and in a letter to me written on February 6th, 1976 he wrote:

"One of these days we might put enough together to publish a book on the subject, anyhow, information is becoming difficult to obtain, and to find an initiate to assist in deciphering it, is now nigh impossible."

He loved and respected the Aborigines and would say, "Forget the drunk you see around Redfern and other cities. Look into their culture, their myths and legends, their paintings, that's where you will find the real Aborigine."

He told me the Tribal Elders approved of his making public their ancient beliefs, as theirs was a problem of communication. Cyril was a blood brother and they wanted him to tell white Australia that the black Australian also had a religious philosophy that was meaningful.

At Groote Eylandt he learned of the next dimension of consciousness which, according to the Aborigines, can be experienced from the physical dimension. This was demonstrated to him on the airstrip when a DC3 was landing, which the Aborigines saw as a great silver bird.

One of the Aboriginal Wisemen was sitting in the jeep beside him. Cyril had been questioning him for some time about where the next dimension of life was and where Aborigines went after physical death. Tapping Cyril on the shoulder this day, he said, "See big, wide bird. See swinging stick", referring to the propeller, "Can see through."

"That's right", Cyril replied. "It goes very fast."

When the plane had landed and stopped the Tribal Elder went on. "See swinging stick, no can see through, that body, that us. When going very fast can see through; that next life."

Sometime later, Cyril was talking to some University students about this and one of them brought up Einstein's theory of relativity and commented. "You know what happens there, don't you. Beyond the speed of light everything loses its length and breadth. There is no gravitation, no time and so on, and it seems to me they may be on to something."

There were times when we discussed the boomerang and both agreed the Aborigines must have known about the science of aero-dynamics thousands of years ago.

Aborigines claim the physical world is connected to a subtle or psychic dimension by character vibrations and that this land of mystery actually exists beyond the speed of light. This is the Dreamtime, so often referred to in Aboriginal mythology, a land where thought is a powerful and potent force, a land where gravitation is non-existent and where time as we know it, stands still.

This is where the ancestral heroes of the Dreamtime reside. It is a psychic dimension, where, in a heightened state of consciousness the Wiseman or Shaman of the tribe makes contact with the Dreamtime ancestors of the spirit world.

Cyril was adamant that their heritage was as important as any other and he would say to me. "The religious philosophy of the Aboriginal people is just as advanced as Christianity, Buddhism or Hinduism and we have it right here in Australia. I don't understand why we treat these people as primitive. After all, they have been on this continent for perhaps as many as 50,000 years. A Tribal Elder gets very upset if you suggest they migrated here from another land. They have always been here. They are the original Australians."

No one can dispute they are the original Australians, even though they were dispossessed, culturally uprooted and denigrated by the white settlers who quickly conquered them and their lands in a type of guerilla warfare.

Land is an important possession of the Aboriginal people. It does not belong to an individual but is shared by the tribe. This tribal ownership of the land and its products is a perpetual inheritance from one generation to another. It cannot be sold, exchanged or transferred. Any such transaction is unthinkable. Full blooded, initiated Aborigines have a personal and spiritual relationship with the land. Removal from it is the cause of the psychological distress and social problems they suffer today.

The land includes the abodes of the pre-existent spirits, sacred grounds, animals and plants of totemic existence. Aborigines, unified by the myths, rituals, legends and traditions of their beginnings ~ The Dreamtime ~ sustained a harmonious co-existence with the environment. They shared the closeness of nature and a direct dependence on it, a preoccupation, not only reflected in mythology, but also in ritual activity.

They saw themselves as an integral part of the physical environment, not something apart from all other living things within it, but having an intimate relationship with them. This relationship and the kind of spiritual identification it involves has been called totemic.

The totem is incarnate in an animal or tree with which the person has some kind of psychic identity. If the totem is that of an animal, the animal itself is considered as some sort of brother to the person. A person whose brother is a crocodile, for instance, is supposed to be safe in crocodile infested areas.

Cyril Havecker's totem was the wombat. According to the Tribal Elders he had been a wombat in his previous life.

An Aborigine feels that the land owns the person. That is why they rarely move from their own tribal land as it takes care of everyone. If it is taken from them, they lose their cultural identity and self-esteem. If it is mined or dug up, they believe it to be a personal physical assault on them. The totemic ties to the land deprives them of personal territorial rights.

Full-blooded Aborigines in their natural state, are deeply religious people. They are not in the same way materially oriented as is the European and this leaves them free to experience a full religious life. When it comes to extra-sensory perception, such as experiencing another dimension, they are keen that we should know about it, too.

These days, there are few full blooded initiated Aborigines left. We long ago confiscated their lands, destroyed their sacred Bora grounds and wiped out their traditional way of life. But when an Aborigine is initiated, he is taught about extra-sensory perception and how to contact the next dimension of existence to get certain information. By so doing, life becomes much easier because he knows the future and can pick up on what has happened in the past.

Cyril was sure they had used this method to overcome Australia's torrid and difficult physical environment for nearly 50,000 years.

"We, as whites, would never have been able to cope with it, and I doubt if we would have survived it at all," he said.

I questioned him about Aboriginal women and the part they played and his response was. "The women know about the Laws of Nature and of the spirit world. Women play an important part in Aboriginal life and are taught about the Mysteries, usually by a head woman, not called a Wise-woman, but nevertheless a wise woman, just the same."

Women initiates have their own ritualistic ceremonies. Their responsibilities include the harmonising of emotions, love magic, maintaining social and cultural harmony, caring for children and the land, and food gathering. The women do not reveal the secrets of their rituals to the men.

In a letter to me dated October 6th, 1975 which accompanied the draft of the first chapter, he wrote.

". . . attached is an attempt to explain the need of the white man and orthodoxy to understand the 'religion' of the Australian black man . . . it is an attempt to answer your request for an explanation of Aboriginal thought, so far as a basic philosophy is concerned. I find it easier to lecture than to write, and it will, no doubt, require your expert editing."

-Yvonne Malykke

Aborigines in Central Australia living a traditional lifestyle

before Europization

ALCHERINGA
(In the Beginning)

Nude, smooth and giant huge,
The torsos of the gums
Hold up the vast, dark cave
As the great moon comes.

The land, the myths go back,
Back to a time unknown
Chaos that had not word
Nor image carved on stone.

-Cyril Havecker

The Creation Myth

TEN THOUSAND YEARS AGO, there occurred in Australia, a disastrous flood which brought famine to the land. Birds, animals and humans survived the rising water by clinging to the mountain ridges. When the waters subsided, cannibalism prevailed amongst remaining humanity.

The Wisemen of the tribe gathered everyone together and directed them to channel their thoughts to the Great Spirit Baiame of whom they had heard from their ancestors and Tribal Elders. They asked Baiame for help, realising that the existing situation could not continue if they were to ensure the survival of their race.

Baiame heard them in the spirit world of Bullima and said to his friends, Nungeena (Mother Nature), Punjel (the Architect of the Universe) and Yhi (Sun Goddess) that something would have to be done to overcome the present crisis on Earth. They agreed.

It was decided that Baiame would manifest on Tya (Earth) as a man, and explain to his creation how to best live in the new environment.

He sent a message by clear sentience and because every animal, plant, mineral and human has a portion of the Great Spirit's Intelligence, and were at the time, highly developed psychically, they were able to receive the Great Spirit's message with ease.

He told them they were to gather at the Moon Lake (Lake Narran), and when Pleiades appeared in the sky, Baiame would manifest.

From across the land came the people, birds and animals. They were drawn, like a magnet to the Moon Lake. There they found a paradise. Lush vegetation, fruits, berries and an abundance of fish. They revelled in the good life while waiting for the most auspicious of moments.

Early one morning, a great whirlwind appeared on the distant horizon. The dust rose up from earth to sky and as it fell again it covered the gathering people by the lake. Whirling in a pyramidal form towards the camp site, it veered off and stopped at the edge of Lake Narran. Out of the whirlwind stepped an Aboriginal man who, with a friendly greeting said. "Fear me not, I am Baiame your Creator and I have come to instruct and help you to overcome your difficulties. Sit down and I will explain what must be done. Make a sacred circle for our meeting, but remember, this sacred circle must never be destroyed or disturbed, as it is now a great energy centre to be utilised by you and your offspring."

They cleared the ground in accordance with the dimensions Baiame gave and made a circle representing his body, out of which comes everything in existence. The sacred circle became known as the Bora Ring.

They worked rapidly preparing the Bora Ring for the evening's Ceremony of Initiation. After preliminary instructions Baiame wandered off into the bush. Night fell. They lit the fires, prepared and ate their meals and again waited. Suddenly, there was an unfamiliar and eerie sound from the bush, proclaiming Baiame's approach to the Bora ground. He carried a piece of wood, oval shaped and tapered at the corners and he said to them. "The sound you hear is the Gayandi or bullroarer. The bullroarer is a sacred object, it calls up the spirit world."

He showed them how to use it by whirling it around the head and explained how it contained the eight notes of the musical scale.

"Now I will tell you why you are here and what your purpose in life is. What I confide to you will serve as your life's philosophy for generations to come, until the end of your race."

They all gathered closer to him to hear what Mysteries and Magic the Great Spirit was about to reveal. He began **The Creation Myth**.

In the beginning, aeons and aeons ago, after previous works, Baiame lay asleep and while sleeping dreamed of life as it was in the past, the present and how it will be in the future.

He got so excited during his dream of the future that it became a nightmare and the body of the universe began to shiver and shake. The vibrations of his body awakened his helpers from a previous time, space and dimension. They were Nungeena, Punjel and Yhi.

When he awoke they were alongside him and Punjel said. "We know you want to create this dream and we will help you to materialise it. I have already been thinking of a similar concept and I have a plan as to how it can be done. It would necessitate the creation of many millions of workers to construct this great edifice of life, and I think we are going to have to do this by taking from your Supreme Intelligence, multi-millions of portions of intelligence which I would like to call yowies (souls) giving them three inherent qualities as well as the power to mould any type of form they desire. However, they will need incentives to do this work and will therefore, need three strong drives.

"First, they must seek nutrition to build and maintain the physical body for continued survival.

"Second, they must be given a sex drive for every species of life to reproduce itself.

"Third, the ambition and desire to achieve.

"These three drives will also be the cause of all the trouble and mischief on Tya, as well as being the cause of all that is positive and productive. Each soul shall have the will and freedom to discriminate between a positive or negative action, their choice of action being dependent upon their inherent wisdom-knowledge and the evolutionary level of each soul."

The three drives were eventually bestowed on each yowie, together with the power to mould form. The cosmic plan for projecting the thought creation to Tya was discussed again and again. Eventually, Punjel put forward the idea of taking the units of intelligence out of the body of Baiame, putting them into a mixing bowl and swirling them around in an anti-clockwise motion. The yowies could then be thought-projected to Tya with a swirling motion which would give the gravitational force required for transference to Earth.

They all agreed this was the best plan for projecting their thought-creation to Earth. So the great mass began to whirl in the body of Baiame, and slowly the plan began to materialise. The yowies began moulding their forms, just as it happened in the Great Spirit's dream.

They began the moulding of primitive form and Tya soon became a solid mass. While Tya was slowly projecting outwards from no thing into form, the hierarchy entered into further discussions about the complexities of their creation.

Realising the responsibility they had bestowed on the yowies by giving them the three drives and the power to mould form, they decided to give them a memory. Otherwise, in time, there would be terrible chaos instead of cosmic order and reason.

Punjel said. "I will give them two other bodies, one in the form of a spirit body or Dowie which will be the container of every individual experience. It will be a memory bank from which they can recollect all previous experiences. This will make their work on Tya easier and will bring order into creation instead of disorder.

"They will also need protection from each other and will require a second and subtle body which I will call the Mullowill. This sheath will protect them from psychic and emotional influences which will build up around them and will be influences of their own making. The Mullowill will also act as a protective sheath for the Dowie."

As Punjel spoke, his plan was taking effect and the memory repository was taking subtle form in the mineral world.

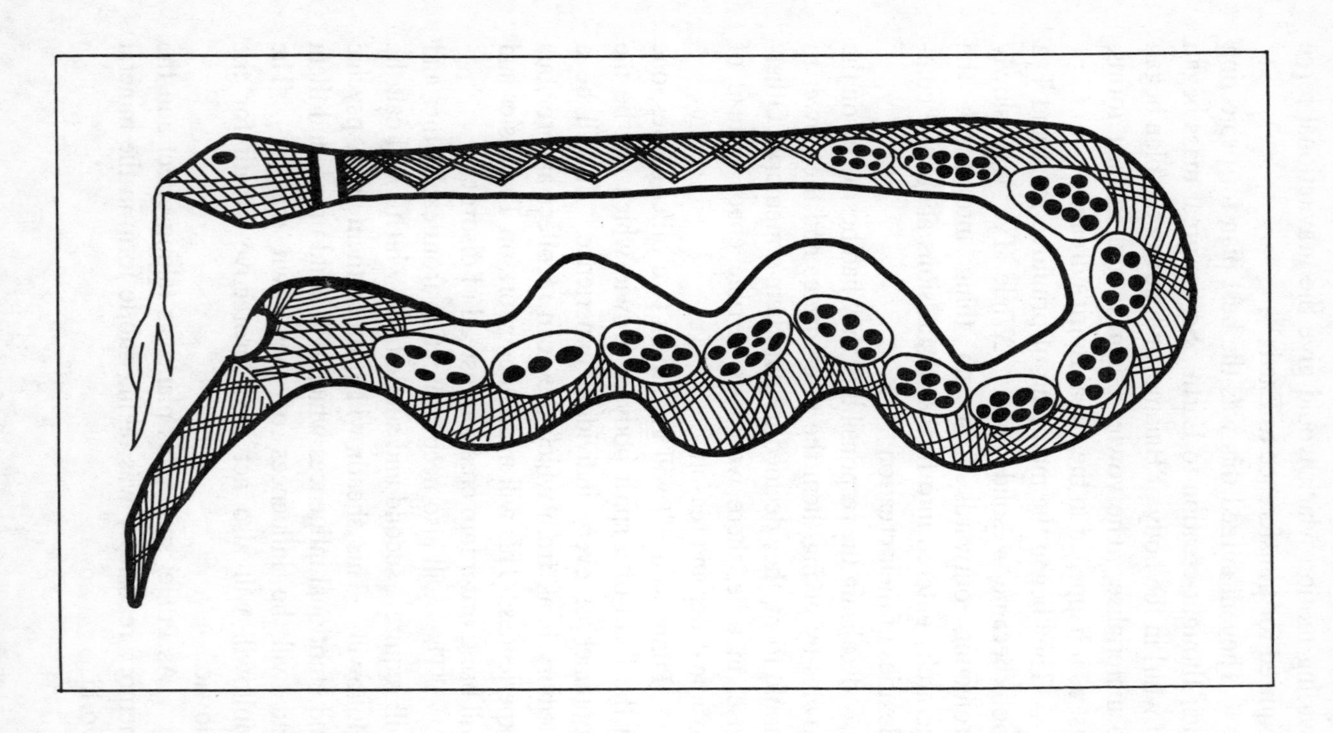

The mythical Rainbow Serpent, symbol of fertility. An ancestral spirit of sacred significance being that of both phallus and womb. It is the father and mother of all forms of life.

The work continued. Tya took shape and solidified even more. After a time, fog enveloped the whole of Tya.

Nungeena was then called upon to do her work in the great creation scheme. The plant world was to be the next stage of creation.

Nungeena realised the yowies did not have much creative ability. Their capacity for creation at their present stage of evolution would only be for lowly mosses and as there was no sunlight, a further problem had to be overcome.

She summoned Punjel and said. "The conditions are not right for the moulding of further plant life as you want it, we must call on Yhi the Sun Goddess for help."

Yhi responded and sent her warming rays to Tya, creating a steam cap and melting the ice which had formed during the aeons of time that had passed.

Ice melted and water covered the Earth causing Nungeena further consternation as she watched her lowly plant life drowning. Again, she called on the hierarchy in the spirit world.

Together they summoned Uluru, the Intelligent Snake from the higher spirit realms of the universe. Instantly, there appeared a great rainbow in their midst and from this rainbow a huge spirit snake slithered to Earth and manifested in form as Uluru, the Great Rainbow Serpent.

He began burrowing holes into the solid earth. These vast holes became the seas, rivers and lakes. This dug out, solid, earth substance became the hills and mountains.

Uluru in his haste, had dug out a vast amount of earthy substance causing Tya to become unbalanced and it began to wobble as it rotated in space. The Rainbow

Serpent panicked and began throwing surplus soil into the air towards Yhi the Sun Goddess, who, seeing it coming towards her, immediately reacted with a command.

"I don't want this substance contaminating me. Stop!" Nungeena, seeing what had happened, asked Yhi.

"What have you done to all the beautiful yowies? Why have you suspended them in space?"

"Don't worry about it, Nungeena, it is only dead earth, rocks and lifeless material which is of no value. The yowies will return to their spiritual bodies. They are not lost. Besides, we cannot keep what is not needed. Surplus matter must be got rid of, otherwise Tya will be overcrowded, unbalanced and disorder and suffering will prevail."

Yhi pondered on what she could do with the lifeless and unwanted refuse suspended in space and decided to call it Bahloo, the Moon and left it there.

All went well for a time, the plant world flourished and for a while everything was in a state of harmony. But, as physical manifestation is, by its very nature, impermanent, changes to the environment were inevitable. This natural law permits life to evolve through varied experiences, even, if at times, the effects might be difficult.

Nungeena, with her motherly love, had nurtured the plant world too much and it began to spoil by overgrowing itself. Again, she turned to Punjel and Baiame for the solution.

"There is war going on in the plant world" she said. "Each species is trying to dominate over the other."

Punjel pointed out that it was the consequence of the three drives. This, coupled with Nungeena's purpose in the scheme of things, ensured the species continued, no matter what the cost.

After lengthy discussions they all decided it was time for animals to be introduced to Tya in the hope of bringing balance to the uncontrollable growth in the plant world. The advanced yowies, having progressed in their evolutionary growth during their life as minerals, were called upon by Punjel to inhabit the forms of the animals, thus controlling the overgrowth of the plant kingdom.

These advanced yowies were selected through the memory bank which was transparent and visible to psychic sight.

Their progress was obvious and showed that the advanced yowies were capable of moulding the eucalyptus, salt bush and other vegetation. They were selected on their creative ability, desire to achieve and reliability.

The yowies began by moulding the form of a jelly-fish and commenced their initial life experience in the ponds and billabongs. Soon they overpopulated and were uniform in appearance.

Nungeena called on Uluru for assistance as she was concerned about the sameness of the species. Together they called upon the rain spirits to bring rain so the rivers would overflow and expand.

If the desire to survive was strong enough, the jelly-fish would have to struggle to overcome the suffering associated with existence. Only the strongest of the species would survive, again to change form and adapt to a new environment.

The plan was to reduce the numbers and make for a stronger, fitter and more developed species. The weaker who failed to adapt to a new environment would lose their form, return to the spirit body and remain in the spirit world to undergo a different type of pain and struggle for the purpose of building character and form.

The hierarchy, after more discussion about the subtle aspects of the plan, finally agreed. Down came the rains, and after a long period the jelly-fish who survived eventually began to adapt to the new environment.

The water animals took up new and various shapes to express their inherent drives and qualities, adjusting over time, to the environment of the age and the locality of their habitat.

Time passed with the stronger trying to dominate over the weaker and Nungeena was again given the task of solving the problem. She created the turtle, who emerged from the water to lay her eggs on the land. From those eggs came the first land animals.

The yowies who hatched out the eggs, after long evolution, gradually took on the form of reptiles, goannas, lizards and snakes and began their own reproductive cycle.

Then came the bunyip who dominated over all and ravaged the land. Again the hierarchy met to discuss how this new problem could be controlled.

The bunyip had a single-chambered heart and disliked cold weather. Aboriginal X-ray drawings depict the heart of the bunyip by a triangle. Uluru brought cold water to the land and slowed down the bunyip. Most of this species perished in the colder climate. However, the change in climate did not prevent other species of life from flourishing.

Aeons of time again passed. Life was harmonious and balanced. Time was now perfect for the finest of all creation. A special creation of enormous complexity. The human.

In Aboriginal philosophy, the soul of a human is the sum total of experiences in all the mineral, plant and animal kingdoms, and when the animal body dies, all the experiences registered in the soul remain impressed on the Dowie.

Punjel thought it a good idea to send from the spirit world, advanced intelligence of animal species to Tya in the form of a higher type of animal, presumably, a gorilla. Baiame and Yhi disagreed, saying this would be a debasement of the finest of all creation.

It was decided to create a man in the spirit form first, then they would mould the form into a shape upon which they would agree unanimously. When the time came for the final moulding, Baiame decided to go to Tya and manifest in human form to explain to the three existing kingdoms of mineral, vegetable and animal that a new companion of greater intelligence, ability and drive than they, would be joining them.

Baiame descended to Tya with his creation of three hundred men and women who became the first tribe. Their spirit bodies comprised all the previous experiences and intelligence of the mineral, plant and animal kingdoms.

Baiame taught them how to live, how to manage the land, how to use a fire stick, the best method for gathering, selecting and cooking food. He taught them the dances and ceremonies of their tribal rites. He taught them the Laws of the Universe and its magic, the art of healing. After a while he created for himself two beautiful and highly intelligent women, as it was not possible for one woman to be accomplished in all the talents he required of them.

Birranooloo was the most intelligent of the two and was chosen to teach the women of the tribe the Laws of Nature and the Laws of the Spirit World. Cannanbeelee taught the women how to cook, produce and raise healthy children and how to maintain social harmony.

She advised that if any babies were born either physically or mentally handicapped it would be wise to dispose of them immediately. If they were to live and reproduce they could, in time, weaken the race and it would eventually disintegrate.

The wise women advised them to organise and control the population in order to meet their needs in an easy and stress free manner.

The women of the first tribe learned about the creation myths and legends, about the Mysteries and Magic of the universe and Baiame became the first Medicineman or Shaman. He selected eight tribal members for a Council of Elders who were made responsible for administering the Laws of the Dreamtime.

One was the most intelligent of hunters, the best honey gatherer, the Wiseman of the tribe and so on. All the tribal Elders were expert in their particular field of accomplishment, and all showed perfect self-determination because of their expertise.

Baiame told them that if they were to show weakness in their individual accomplishments or digress from the Laws of Nature and the Laws of the Spirit World by adopting a way of life foreign to the social and religious structure he had taught them, this would mean the dissolution of their race.

Baiame manifesting on Tya.

"Any race who borrows from another tradition is doomed to suicide," he said.

Finally, Baiame returned to the spirit world and his superior creation progressed and lived in harmony until the great flood, when once again the Tribal Elders called upon him to help them overcome their present crisis on Tya.

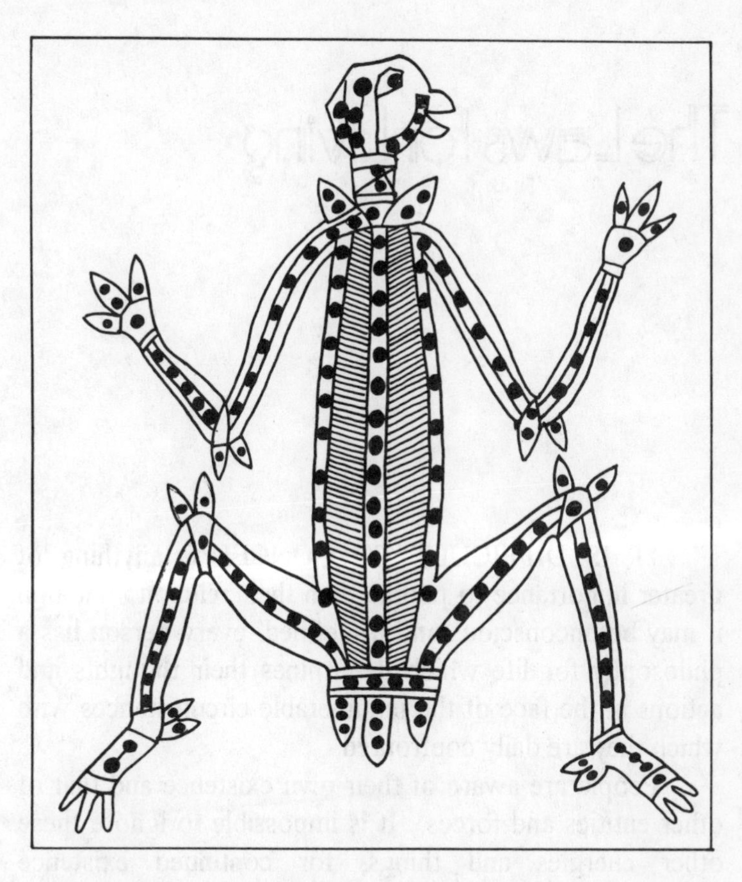

Marrgon, the ancestral spirit of thunder and lightning. Stone axes embedded in the knees, shoulders, elbows and ankles, split rocks and trees when lightning strikes.

The Laws for Living

IT IS DIFFICULT TO CONCEIVE anything of greater importance to people than their religion. Though it may be unconscious and ill-defined, every person has a philosophy for life which determines their thoughts and actions in the face of the innumerable circumstances with which they are daily confronted.

People are aware of their own existence and that of other entities and forces. It is impossible to ignore these other energies and things, for continued existence demands that they be recognised. Due allowance must be made for their values as life-supporting and life-destroying factors.

Each person then, is constantly called upon to make adjustments with which to meet the requirements of contact with other persons, entities and forces. The nature of the adjustment depends upon a person's ideology for life, be it conscious or unconscious. Although we may be inclined to reject the term, it can, in its broadest sense, be termed our religion. So it is with the Australian Aborigine. They live in, and are influenced by, both the physical and spiritual world.

For centuries religious orthodoxy has kept the western world behind an iron curtain of ignorance. It no longer resorts to the violence of the Inquisition, but nevertheless maintains a barrier which prevents people from learning the facts. In their impressionable childhood people are taught they should not make investigation into religion. Rather, they are encouraged to place reliance on blind belief to keep them behind an iron curtain of ignorance. The practice threatens them with misunderstanding and often suffering.

Having set the date of creation, Church Law did all in its power to withhold and discredit the records of the rocks and evidence of early humanity. Primitive humans lived later than 4000 BC according to orthodoxy, yet the Australian Aborigine is known to have existed for more than 40,000 years.

It is not surprising then, that humanity in the past had erroneous ideas about itself, the Earth and about life after physical dissolution. Nor, at the present day, do we possess entire information on these subjects. The intention here is not to criticise the ignorance of the past or that of today, but is mentioned to show how ignorance, misunderstanding and fear ~ for which orthodoxy can be held responsible ~ has impeded investigation. People have felt free to question and explore and so realise for themselves facts which are essential for their continued well-being and progress.

Two rainmaking spirits, Wuluwaid and Bunbulama, they carry magic bundles in their hands. A rainbow is depicted about their heads and rain is seen falling about them. They live in the spirit world.

It is important that the shackles of orthodoxy be lifted if the white person is to understand the black person and for them both to live to advantage. The penetration of standard belief has always been difficult even where the physical world is concerned, but discernment of the spiritual world, every bit as important ~ particularly to the Australian Aborigine who lives among a world of spiritual beliefs ~ is an even harder task.

Instead of possessing some foggy notion as to what religion is, people should understand that today, as in the past, it is their effort to employ non-physical means to find on Earth ample satisfaction for their existence. The drive, in other words, for nutrition, reproduction and for significance and to find satisfaction for these three drives for as long as possible in the spiritual world.

In an expanded form, the Australian black person believes that the drive for nutrition embraces all means of survival. The urge for reproduction includes mental creation, as well as physical progeny, whilst the desire for significance encompasses the various means of expression.

Dreamtime

Knowledge, to the Aborigine, was derived from experience, and to be of value it must be correctly interpreted.

The Aborigines, through the appointed wise men and women, gradually acquired information about both the physical and the spiritual environment, from advice handed down from one generation to the next by word of mouth. Sometimes the communication was poor and the interpretation erroneous because the information that could be handed down orally was limited. It was bound by the experience of the individual, who often sought to make it the property of the tribe, and it was limited by the ability of members of the tribal hierarchy to remember what they had been told.

With the accumulation and application of knowledge gained over thousands of years, the crude pictographs which the black people had used to convey ideas and refresh memories gradually developed into rock and bark paintings. Illustrations were kept as permanent records in the form of recognised symbolism embracing periods in time not recognised by orthodoxy. These permanent records aided the black person in their acquisition of knowledge and have been referred to as the *Dreamtime*, the history of many generations of the Australian Aboriginal people, records of incalculable significance and importance which the white people, through ignorance, have chosen to destroy.

The Aborigines knew that a person must obtain experience and knowledge in order to further their progress towards improved nutrition, increased benefits for offspring and greater significance. The only hope of bettering conditions was to learn all that was possible about both the physical and spiritual worlds and the laws operating in these environments. The Laws for Living were laid down by the Creator, an all pervading Super-Intelligence known to all of the initiated as Baiame.

The story of the creation has a special significance in the life of the Aborigines, for it reveals the beginning of the universe itself, laws to be adopted for optimum living here on Tya, the Earth, and in the next life, beyond the physical.

In analysing the story, it must be understood that Baiame is the first spiritual substance from which all physical matter, as we know it, is composed; the body of the universe and something pervading all materials and space, even that which, to our senses, seems empty; an intelligence of incalculable grades, non-physical in nature, which transmits heat, light, chemical energy and electricity. All life began, in response to the psychokinetic power of images within the mind of this great spirit. In effect, the universe was created as the result of a thought image, or mental picture, which became the plan for life for all living things.

The will to put the image into something tangible was so great, that it set into motion the elements of this first spiritual substance, which, in turn, gradually materialised to form the universe. When there is no spiritual desire, there can be no organic activity of any kind. Under the jurisdiction of this powerful force, lesser intelligences of the spirit (often referred to in Aboriginal mythology) would perform psychokinetic functions. They are described as the Nature Spirits. All living things, according to the wise men and women, have at least three spiritual bodies, all of which are necessary in the cycle of existence.

The Yowie, or soul, that incarnates in human form, has evolved from innumerable lower forms of life, at each step gaining new experiences which enable it to be attracted to and successfully build about itself a higher form. It is the conscious mind, the character and the unconscious mind all bound together as one. The real "I" if you like, of every living thing ~ the aggregate of all experiences at any given time. The soul never leaves the body of the living except at physical death, when it goes to reside permanently on the Dowie.

Dowie

The Dowie is the next life so far as we human beings are concerned. It is built of substance that is frictionless, but retains indefinitely all of the motions imparted to it. In this sense, it is thought built and of a velocity greater than the speed of light. Inhabited by all kinds of entities and forms of life, the Dowie is not somewhere in space, it is all about us and it requires only the proper conditions to be contacted at any given time. We know, of course, that this subtle substance does not communicate motion directly to physical substance. The difference in velocity between the two dimensions seems to be too great for such a direct contact. The two substances are separated by the Mullowill (etheric sheath) that surrounds the body of all living things. Damage to the Mullowill, the Shaman will explain, can cause mental disease and even death.

While ordinary people have very little control over the Dowie, other than receiving the occasional "flash", message, or premonition, of some past or future event, the dimension can be contacted by a proper mental technique which is worthy of mention. A directed thought, or an electrical message can be passed from the physical brain, through the Mullowill to the receiving spiritual brain located in the Dowie. The process is reversed when the message is returned. In actual fact, it can be likened to the transmitting and receiving of radio messages.

Aboriginal Shaman are well known for their powers in extra-sensory perception and control of the mind.

Provided the correct vibration or wave length ~ compatible with that in the spiritual world ~ is obtained, contact between the two worlds can become regular practice. The teaching can be understood more readily when we appreciate that the protoplasm of the physical body exists in the form of cells. In a like manner, the psychoplasm of the Dowie is not a homogeneous mass, but exists in the form of innumerable cells which can be best described as thought cells.

Aboriginal teaching is that "all things only alter by degree". By using that formula as a basis, it is not difficult to comprehend that the Dowie is simply something progressed further than its physical counterpart. But because they only alter in structure one can be in contact with the other. In summarising to this point, we have discovered some very interesting teachings in the "religion" of the Aborigines. To begin with, it can be assumed that the world we live in is a mental creation, a body of spirit loaded with all kinds of potential. That we, as the "cells" or workers, help to make up this great body of Baiame. It is a planned creation and all living things are brought into existence with the object of fulfilling a function in the great plan for life. Guidelines, or laws for living have been laid down by the Creator, and to achieve optimum living it is necessary for all forms of life to understand and apply them to the environment of the day.

The realisation that every form of life has a soul, and at least three bodies or dimensions, leads us to believe that extra-sensory perception, the future after physical death, and constant contact with the much more knowledgeable spiritual world, are all accepted facts.

A kinship amongst the cells, or all living things, becomes essential for the body of Baiame to function properly. And if we are to again apply the teaching that "all things only alter by degree", we can assume that our own physical bodies are but a replica of that of the universe adapted to the environment of the day.

Initiation

The Laws for Living are given to each Aboriginal youth at the time of his or her initiation, or the period of education which fits them for adulthood. Many thousands of years ago ~ the wise man or woman will tell you ~ because it was necessary to acquaint all things with the laws of living and fulfil the great plan for life, Baiame manifested into the physical form of a man.

On arrival, all things of intelligence were called together to attend the first Bora, or sacred ceremony, and instructed in the Laws of the Universe. This was the first initiation ceremony, the format of which has been carried on from generation to generation, right up to the present day. Is it any wonder then that the elders of the Aboriginal tribes have seen fit to challenge the confiscation of the lands on which these sacred places exist? The act amounts to the destruction of the equivalent of St. Mary's Cathedral, or some such sacred house of prayer. The fulfilment of the great plan for life meant that its realisation could only be possible through the exercise of highly specialised talents and through the use of abilities that are not the same in detail as those of any other Yowie or soul.

These abilities can be acquired only through a suitable education. It has been suggested that the

Australian black is primitive and uneducated, but in the environment of the bush land and desert wastes they have been able to overcome extreme conditions and survive. They are surviving today because of their philosophy and they will adapt, despite the frustrations brought about by the failure of the white people to understand their problem of the hurried change in environment.

The teaching of "Progress or Perish" is very much alive in the mind of the black person. It is the Law of Nature that all living things must comprehend if they wish to survive in this, or any dimension of existence. All life forms, whatever they may be, have obstacles to overcome, suffer pain, enjoy pleasure and must struggle to adjust themselves to an ever-changing environment.

In the teachings of the black person, the type of experience attracted by either a human or a snake is not determined in moral worth, nor meted out as a reward or punishment. It is attracted because that person or that snake requires that particular experience to teach it something which it must know if it is to fulfil its eternal destiny. If the lesson is not learned from one experience of a kind, it will continue to attract that type of experience until it does learn. Whatever, the experiences which the life form undergoes at any particular time may be pleasurable or painful, because the Yowie or soul has the need for them in its growth. The acquisition of knowledge, like everything else, depends on a proper beginning and the wise person chooses the only true teacher ~ Nature.

Baiame is not always correct in what is created at the first attempt. It is often necessary for the elimination of a species or thing which upsets progress. The creatures of the bush land, which again only alter in degree to a human being, show how Nature will take care of the problem. Organisms need each other. Few living things can survive for long without the living group and the living community.

The Laws of Nature

It is because of this natural law that the Australian black people insist on universal kinship and welfare. They find it difficult to understand why they are put aside by the white people. But then we have not been educated by example in these kinds of things. We are ignorant of the facts clearly visible in the great laboratory of Nature. Social life offers advantages in fulfilling two important needs in Nature ~ food and safety. Yet such an attitude in the community may not seem neighbourly. How can we have a community and eat it?

Foxes depend on rabbits for food and so keep the number of rabbits in check. A limited population of rabbits in turn imposes a limit on the number of foxes. The human being is a natural predator, living on the meat of mammals, fish and poultry, as well as plants. All living things are in constant search for nourishment. Only if a blade of grass is eaten by a cricket, which in turn is eaten by a frog, which is eaten by a snake and the snake becomes the prey of a kookaburra on high, only then, will the kookaburra find the supply of sunborn energy stored in the blade of grass. The laboratory of nature has so much to offer. It shows that chemical substances that support life circulate in great cyclic paths through the plant and animal community.

The Science of Ecology might point out some of the hazards of over-population amongst Nature. But 40,000 years ago ecology did not exist as a science, nor even as a word, so that the shrewd Aboriginal wise person was quick to realise and use this means for studying life habits and applying the findings to their own environment.

The natural Laws of the Universe remain, whether they be for the plant, animal, humans or the spirits. There is no changing them. They are there today, as they were 40,000 years ago, open to investigation; ready to be applied to the environment of the day. Thirty thousand years of study by the black people means nothing to us. We do not seem to want any advice they have to offer. Religious fundamentalism has smothered anything their investigations offer as being primitive, out of date and unacceptable.

The Laws for Living laid down by the Creator to the original Australian black people seem to have been lost, but the wise people are adamant that they cannot change. If asked why, they will simply tell you, "because Baiame says so, he big fellow, he knows". All of these laws, in most instances, remain occult. Occultism, to the orthodox, is something evil, a kind of black magic, not to be tampered with by any human being.

Occultism is the science of understanding subtle forces, and the art of subjecting them to human control. They are not directly apprehended by the five ordinary senses upon which the physical scientist relies for all knowledge. The line of demarcation between that which is called occult is, therefore, constantly changing, for every now and then scientists invent a device by which some hitherto subtle force is made directly perceptible to the physical senses. It is then no longer considered occult. It is clear, then, that the common application of the word 'occult' ~ since it depends upon the experience of the speaker, for what is hidden to one may be perceived by another, is wholly arbitrary.

The word certainly carries with it an air of mystery, it is true, but all forces are mysterious to those who have not studied them and what is mysterious to the ignorant is obvious to the learned. Yet, in all Nature, nothing can come permanently under this ban for all mysteries may be solved. All things, according to Natural Law, obey those by which they manifest, and while these laws remain incomprehensible, any phenomenon will seem mysterious. We fear that which we do not understand, but with understanding comes courage. With knowledge we see how any hidden danger, if there is danger, can be circumvented. Surely this is a message that both the white and black people ought to comprehend, that is, to understand each other's philosophy of life and religion because a person's only progression here and hereafter must be founded on knowledge. Only by this means can we expect to subjugate our environment and enjoy its opportunities.

So it is with things spiritual. For only through a knowledge of Spiritual Law can we mould our spiritual environment and enjoy spiritual powers while on Tya, the Earth.

The Aboriginal wise person makes no claim to infallibility. They do, however, present the views of their people, who after at least 40,000 years of study into the Laws of Nature and the changing environment of this country, believe that they have something to offer the community. Should, then, this learning and research be discredited by orthodoxy, or should agreeable effort be made to understand it?

Love and wisdom, the answer to overcoming racism, can only be achieved by experience, knowledge and truth.

The Wirinun induces emotion with the whirring, shrieking sound made by the Gayandi. The sound vibration made during a ritual ceremony summons ancestral beings.

Aboriginal Magic

RAINMAKING CEREMONIES, FAITH HEALING, THE POINTING OF THE BONE and so on, all fall into this category of strange occurrences.

The objects of our environment, for example, radiate an energy which has an influence upon our lives. The thoughts of living people impinge upon our consciousness. Under certain circumstances, people who have passed on can contact us. Beside thought, actions of people also have a suggestive force. Astrological energies also stimulate our thoughts and actions and there is the subject of ceremonial magic which is employed almost daily by one person or another with the use of charms, birthstones or talismans of some kind.

All of these influences, though imponderable, may nevertheless exert an influence upon human life. They are used by the Wirinun or Aboriginal medicineman (Shaman) and play an important role in the existence of every Australian Aborigine.

Magic, including that of the Aborigines, is worthy of investigation because so long as an effect is produced by an unknown force shrouded in mystery, there is apt to be an excessive reverence or fear. The best way to remove excessive reverence or fear is not to deny the effect, but to find out just how it is produced. The most powerful of all imponderable forces to influence our lives ~ according to the Wirinun ~ are our Kungullun, or thoughts.

That thought is a powerful influence in shaping human life and destiny is purported to be one of the lessons taught by the great spirit and projector of the universe ~ Baiame ~ at the first initiation ceremony, held in the Alcheringa, or Dreamtime.

The Wirinun or Aboriginal Shaman

Any Aborigine may practise magic, but it is the Wirinun who is regarded as the expert. He is thoroughly trained in his profession. He undergoes a very strong personal discipline, which involves long periods of isolation, restriction in diet, as well as intense study into the Laws of Nature and the spiritual world. He is skilled in faith healing and extra-sensory perception, which makes him a medium of contact between the physical and spiritual dimensions of life.

In regular journeys to the Dowie or subtle world, he is said to contact ancestral beings who have passed on from their physical bodies. He does this in order to obtain past and future information beneficial to the livelihood of the tribe. He is held in high esteem by members of the tribe and occupies an elevated position among the other wise men and elders, responsible for the welfare of the community.

Shaman are not usually sorcerers nor workers of black magic as many writers suggest, indeed they do not work for any material gain whatsoever. While they may employ the practice of "sleight of hand", or some other form of illusion in faith healing "operations", the magic produced is purely psychic and for the good of the other person. The Wirinun practises according to the Laws of Nature and what is believed to have been laid down for the good of the environment by Baiame, the Supreme Intelligence. Induced emotion and directed thought are probably the two most powerful magical "weapons" used by the Wirinun and are worthy of closer examination.

Baiame teaches that the Universe is a mental creation projected out of spirit essence. This concept makes the origins of the phenomenal world mental, with spirit as its essence. It could be called electromagnetic energy manipulated by thought in accordance with Cosmic Law.

The Power of Thought

A thought can be best described as a set of vibratory frequencies within the Dowie. If these vibratory frequencies are transmitted through electromagnetism to the physical brain, the thought rises from the unconscious into the region of objectivity. The individual is then objectively conscious of a thought that may have been present for either a long or short time, in the unconscious, without being aware of it.

If there is a sensation coming from the physical world, the vibratory rates of the brain which are set into motion are then transmitted through the electromagnetism to the Dowie or subtle brain, where they are registered and compared with other rates of motion set up by previous experiences.

Such a comparison, when it rises into objective consciousness through its motions being transmitted to the physical brain, is said to be a definite perception. The force at any given time depends upon the intensity of the thought. The vividness depends upon the ability of the thinker to separate the factors of which the thought is composed. This is accomplished through concentration. The intensity, however, depends upon the number of separate, mental factors utilised, the energy contained in each, and the completeness with which they are joined to act as a single organisation of thought energy.

So it is that mental force results from utilising the experiences of life as integrative factors in the process of building clear-cut mental pictures. If such a force is to result in physical phenomena, or is in any way to operate directly upon physical substance, it must be vitalised with electromagnetic energy. Thought is a force that may be used for good or evil, and is a potent weapon for black magic, as well as a healing aid when administered for well-being.

In Aboriginal teaching, all life began in response to the psychokinetic power of images within the mind of the all-pervading Super-intelligence and Creator ~ Baiame. The universe was formed as a result of a definite image which radiated the energy to create. For a thought to be effective from a magical standpoint, it must be clear cut and strongly energised. The carrying power of a thought and the amount of work it can accomplish depends upon the energy associated with it. A thought which is associated with any emotion whatever has considerable ability to perform. It has considerable "horsepower" and is used to advantage by the Shaman in all magic works.

Ceremonial Magic

The ceremonial factor in magic is not a simple one and to understand its functions we must consider the relationship of the Dowie or subtle world, the Dowie of humans and the Dowie of psychic entities, to magic in general. Magic, if worthy of the name, utilises forces of the Dowie world even though such forces are limited according to the power of the psychic energies of the Wirinun or Shaman. Further, we must recognise that what is built upon the Dowie by the mental imagery of an entity, either incarnate of disincarnate, has an actual and real existence in this spirit world. Under suitable conditions of contact with the physical existence, it manifests here on Tya, the Earth.

An example of the works of the Dowie is illustrated in aboriginal legend by the Wandjina or creative spirits who are concerned with perpetuating the seasons and the rain. They wandered across the land designing the topography. At the end of their work, they went to various caves and left the imprint of their physical bodies on the walls, where their power remains. They then returned to the Dowie dimension of existence. Through a certain ritual, which includes the repainting of the bodies upon the cave walls, the Wirinun can actually contact these entities and ask for assistance in bringing rain. Help will, and does come.

This means that once the thought takes form in the Dowie sphere, and if it makes contact with the psychic forms of those in the physical world, it gains a suitable supply of electromagnetic energy giving it the power to mould and shape the physical environment and influence circumstances to coincide with the Dowie or psychic state. To work anywhere in the universe, to build anything or make a request to the spirit dimension of existence, there must always be a sufficient supply of energy as nothing can be accomplished without consuming energy. The enterprise required for this work is both mental and emotional in character. The emotional property of a thought is especially important, as thought without genuine emotion is of low energy content.

Induced Emotion and Directed Thought

An important function of ceremony and ritual magic is a forceful output of emotion, which is the energy needed for all magical acts. Initiative alone is not sufficient to build a house or bridge, but must be directed into selected channels to be effective. In building a house or bridge, it must be directed along the lines laid down in the plans and specifications. To perform any magical function, energy must receive a specific direction and must be guided accurately into such channels that work towards the desired end. The function of the ceremony of magic can best be described as directed thought, which guides the strong energies of the powerfully induced emotion into the proper channels, causing them to labour for the anticipated result.

The dreaded form of Aboriginal magic called the pointing of the bone is an example of the use of induced emotion and directed thought. This act of magic was given the name because a selected and especially prepared bone or some other substrate, charged with power through chants and directed thought, is pointed at the victim with the object of destroying his or her body.

When the Wirinun jerks the bone in the direction of the victim, ritual singing begins. The emotions and thoughts of those participating are aroused to a high pitch. The victim is made aware that the bone has been pointed by ensuring it is left in a place where the victim will find it. The victim is now detached from all tribal activity. Directed thought, loaded with the death dealing properties of the bone, takes over and the victim knows he or she is doomed. Gradually they become ill, turn morose, begin to waste away, and finally die. At no time has the victim been physically handled and death is due to mental powers alone, or if you like, the magic powers of the Wirinun.

The victim can be saved by directing the death dealing properties of the thought into another direction. By so doing, the powerful thought can be neutralised effectively. However, the new thought must be to cure with enough faith in order that the person will live effectively. This tunes the vibratory rate to a higher frequency and shuts off thoughts that are pernicious. This is easier said than done, for once the powerful energies of thought are channelled into a certain direction they can be likened to a cyclone and are difficult to divert from the set course.

Contacting Invisible Help

If a physical object is too heavy to be moved we call for assistance. So it is with the Wirinun who will call on the spirit entities to assist him with the work of magic in hand. The kind of help enlisted, of course, depends upon the type of work to be executed. The Wirinun, through proper training in concentration and environment of the spirit world, knows the signs, symbols and incantations necessary to call up the psychic entities required.

Each one of them has a definite vibratory rate. That is, to give exclusive attention to a particular entity he tends to tune in on the entity's vibratory rate. If the tuning in process is complete, then it makes for a possible exchange of energies with the entity thought about. It is rather like using a telephone. The Wirinun dials a number or vibratory tone in the Dowie and speaks about the work to be accomplished.

It is true that unusual and startling phenomena can be produced with the aid of elementals. It is of interest that the Wirinun when engaged in important sacred work uses the Bora grounds. The Bora ground consists of two round cleared areas, one larger than the other, generally located in bush land. Although there are several opinions as to what they actually represent, there is no doubt that whilst operating in these sacred areas, the Shaman is protected and immune from evil doers. It is rather like the advice of the Old Book of Magic which informs us that a double circle drawn about a magician will protect him from demons.

Ancestral beings, elementals or other non-human entities are often called upon to help in faith healing because of their knowledge in these matters. Their vast accumulation of knowledge is believed to be of great assistance in the accomplishment of white magic ~ the magic that benefits society as a whole, as a benevolent thought, and evokes a spirit of loving kindness. Fine thoughts and desires promote a sympathetic response; black magic brings evil and the wrath of Baiame, the Supreme Intelligence. The Wirinun will never admit to having practised any form of black magic.

White Magic

The Wirinun never calls upon any spiritual entity with which he is not completely familiar. He must know their nature and aims. He often uses Narmingatha or prayers. These prayers are directed to Baiame, or the ancestral beings of creation that he believes in, that is, the intelligences of the Universe who are of a very high order.

The thought of the Great Spirit or the ancestral beings tend to tune the vibrations of the Wirinun offering it in prayer to the level corresponding to the noble qualities attributed to it. There may be individuals, departed ones, upon whom, in stress, he may call and not infrequently he will receive much needed assistance or advice. In the performance of a task or the attainment of some worthy end, he can enlist the aid of the appropriate ceremony. Dowie energies are at their maximum potency through the employment of some ceremony. But in seeking the aid of benign entities of the spiritual world he uses no words of compulsion, conjuration or extravagant terms.

He simply asks the invisible person the favour he wishes in very much the same words as he would if that person were still here on Tya. He asks earnestly and gives the reason for asking, even as he would to one here on Tya. As the entity is supposedly kindly disposed and quite just, he is not foolish enough to ask for something that deprives someone of what justly belongs to another or which gives an unmerited advantage over someone else. The constant reference to universal kinship and welfare amongst the Shamans is impressive. There is never anything dogmatic about their approach to love and wisdom. It comes through experiencing good and bad. Experience leads to knowledge and eventually to love and wisdom. The Laws of Nature and the Universe are eventually learned by every living soul.

For magical work of much importance, there is usually a preparatory period of considerable duration in which by fasting, chastity and other strict austerities the Wirinun transforms his mind to perform the work contemplated.

Gayandi

It is not infrequent for the performance of some magical process to use the Gayandi or bullroarer to induce emotion. The Gayandi or bullroarer consists of a flat, oval-shaped piece of wood suspended from a string at one end. It is twirled around and around to make a shrill sound which becomes louder and almost ear-splitting as it gathers pace. It is said to set up vibrations that will warn not only physical, but ancestral begins, that magical work is pending. The word Gayandi means the spirit of the Bora or sacred ground. It is a sacred object and must be kept well hidden and used only during important ceremonies.

Like the Tjuringa, which are generally carved or painted pieces of wood or stone and closely associated with the spiritual world, they are held in reverence. Indeed, their hiding places were so sacred that a hunted animal that took refuge there would be safe from harm.

Wandjina. Ancestral beings of the spirit world who are regularly contacted by the Wirinun prior to the wet season. The paintings of these figures are refurbished by a ritual, prior to contact. They are the mythical beings who originally created part of the country and left their likeness imprinted on cave walls before returning to the spirit world. They can be reached by correct thought vibrations.

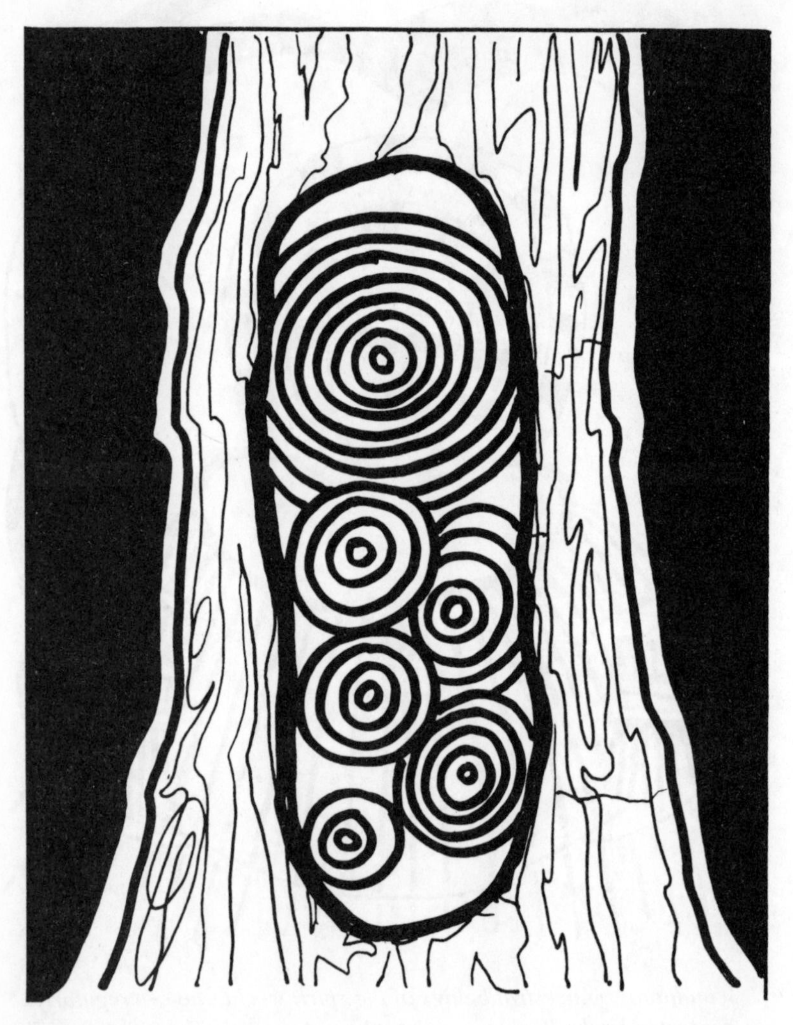

Carved trees with designs of significance, sometimes found near sacred Bora grounds.

These sacred objects have a special vibratory rate which has an affinity with the thought cells of the owner's Dowie. The more active a group of thought cells are, the more power they have, so that, working from the psychic world, they bring desired events into the life of the owner. The Wirinun, in gauging their importance, points out that the frequency with which the sacred object is thought about; the thought power of the individual thinking about them; and the directness with which the thought is sent; all enter into calculations. In any case, they form a bond between the spiritual and physical worlds and are used in adjusting the mind prior to any kind of meditation or deep concentration.

Every act of the preparatory period performed according to the predetermined schedule, drives home into the unconscious mind that a certain result is going to be obtained. As a result of the preparation period, the Wirinun enters into the actual magical act with all of his energy concentrated to give a terrific impact to the accomplishment of his work. Consequently, he is able to do what under normal circumstances would be quite impossible.

The physical brain has very little power to handle the electromagnetic energies which make magical processes of any kind possible. Cerebral concentration tends to generate electrical frequencies which are not suitable for either spiritual activities or the production of physical phenomena.

For use in white magic, the electrical frequencies generated by the nervous system while the mind is in a state of exaltation are most suitable. They not only tune the Wirinun in on spiritual levels which are constructive in character, but they readily become converted into energies which permit the Yowie or soul to become highly active in the spiritual world.

The work accomplished by magical procedure always brings about some change in the Dowie spheres and to bring about this change the Yowie needs to be active in that dimension of existence. If its attention is concentrated on physical interest through continuing habitual thoughts about them, it is unlikely to be active enough on the Dowie dimension to direct the energies towards bringing about the psychic changes necessary for the required results. To change the pattern of a physical object or condition, it is best that cerebral thinking cease. The Yowie must abandon its close attachment to the physical body and move into the Dowie world to do the work.

When the essential pattern of the physical object or condition has been changed, it exercises extra physical power making electromagnetic energy available for the work in hand. The thought cells within each of us employ the same principle to attract into our lives various events, all of which seem so amazing to those who have been educated into the tradition of material science.

It is termed psychokinetic. It is a practice that has been used by the Wirinun for some 40,000 years or more.

The Wirinun's Advice

In all magical matters it ought now be recognised that effects produced, either good or bad, depend upon the impact of the Dowie energies. These energies can only affect a human being when they establish sufficient rapport with his or her subtle dimension. Unless unduly negative, people have the power within themselves to prevent the formation of these conditions. When they have cultivated concentrated thinking to any degree, they are able to turn their attention to whatever matters they desire to think about. If they completely turn their inner and outer attention to some elevating subject, to some pleasant emotion, or to some problem requiring concentration, they automatically destroy all rapport with vibrations of a destructive nature.

Kaldowamp kungullun boorala wanye tumpinyer yackatoon ~ always think good then life will be happy, says the Wirinun. *Annin nglelurumi gelane* ~ have faith brother. *Kungullun motong thure* ~ think strong and straight.

To accomplish anything means having control over body, energies and thoughts. To be unusually accomplished in any direction means that an unusual amount of control has been gained over some set of muscles, some mental process or both. Control over self is the first requisite for success.

The phenomenon that is commonly called magic, is simply the exercise of thought power to influence another person's thoughts and actions without the intervention of the spoken word or of any sign.

Control of our faculties and self is mastership, which is the making of the Wirinun and which gives them the power of imponderable forces of magic.

Tjuringa. Carved or painted pieces of wood or stone associated with totemic ancestors and regarded as sacred. They are talismans of the Alcheringa.

Totemism

WHILE TOTEMISM IS A WIDESPREAD BELIEF among the dark-skinned people of the world, there has been a good deal of conjecture as to the part it plays in the life of the Australian Aborigine and theories have been advanced by many anthropologists and writers who have researched the subject. Totemism, they suggest, is a religion, with social aspects and perhaps an extension of animism or fetishism. Others claim it to be nothing more than superstitious nonsense. As a religion, it is a system of mutual help and protection; in the social scheme, a method by which members of a totem can help and protect one another.

Primitive people believed not only in the existence of the spirits of their ancestors, but also in elemental spirits. Among those people there would be some clairvoyants able to see non-human entities. No doubt they would at times over-estimate the importance they played in natural phenomena, but we cannot be certain what part these elementals perform in wind, rain, lightning and other physical forces. The American Hopi Indians through the "snake dance" are able to contact their friends in the spiritual world and procure help in such cases as warding off drought. Frequently, it has been reported that spectators of this impressive ceremony in an arid region are drenched with rain before they reach home.

Just how psychokinesis operates to produce or protect from natural phenomena or to what extent it has power over them still awaits investigation.

The conditions and laws governing psychic phenomena are so little understood that it is probable that primitive people also failed to grasp fully the means by which elementals are able to produce physical results. No doubt their prayers to these spirits, which they conceived to be behind natural happenings, often fail to bring results. But also, it is quite possible, especially when persons are involved who have considerable natural psychokinetic ability, that occasionally actual results follow earnest efforts to contact these entities.

There are plenty of people today who believe that through earnest prayer they can be protected from injury. Some of these people cite very convincing instances to support their belief. Therefore, until evidence is collected about the power of psychokinesis to render protection, we must not accuse any so-called primitive race of having an altogether vicious superstition.

All life is struggling for survival so that it can continue to express itself. Primitive people were convinced that through their deceased relatives visiting them there was some kind of survival beyond the physical.

It was quite natural they should try to find a way to live on Earth which would assure them of continued life both here and after they had left the material world. They sought means by which in an after life the drive for nutrition, reproduction and significance, which had been the moving power behind all progress of life on Earth, could continue. They had to adapt themselves through understanding and employing spiritual energies in order to find satisfaction for the three irrepressible drives after physical dissolution which came to be called, in later time, their religion.

Religion should not remain static; it ought to develop and progress indefinitely. The aim of religious philosophy, whether so recognised by those who embrace it or not, is to afford optimum living. To obtain the best kind of living, every effort must be made to acquire as many new and significant facts as possible about the physical and spiritual worlds. When they are discovered they ought to be included in their proper relation to all of the data already known. Totemism, it would seem, embraces all of these motives and apparently satisfied the Aboriginal way of life in Australia for many thousands of years.

Animism

Animism is defined as the belief that spirit occupies a person's body. Animistic people believe that birds, beasts, plants, insects and even stones have invisible doubles. The fact that they actually do is being verified by scientific physical researchers today. If the ghosts of dogs and horses manifest to so-called civilised people why should

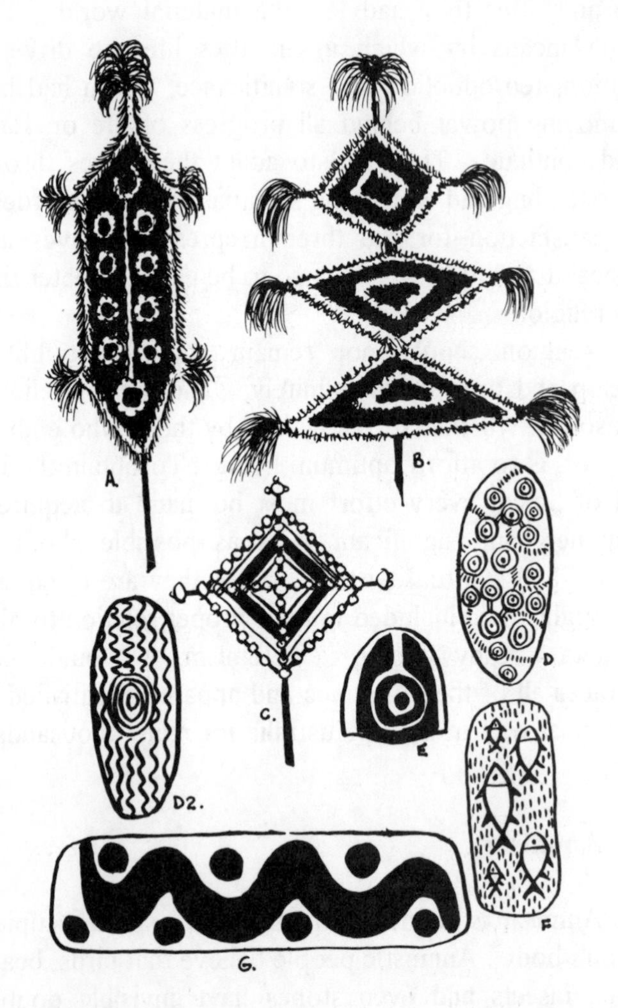

Some Aboriginal Totems: A-Night bird. B-Spider. C-Bird. D-Ant. D2-Waterlily. E-Head-dress. F-Fish. G-Snake.

not the apparitions of other animals be seen by the Aborigines?

Animism proposes that behind material manifestation, objects are invisible and perhaps intelligent forces use these things for expression. Furthermore, it peoples the world with spirits of various kinds, which, although unseen, nevertheless under certain circumstances exert an influence upon human life.

In 1901, A.M. Risley reported his belief that animism existed in its lowest form as the religion of the jungle dwellers of Chota Nagpur, India. He reported that the various spirits which are there are indeterminate in nature and not represented by a symbol of any type. He reported that all over Chota Nagpur there are sacred groves where these spirits, which have not yet been given individual attributes, are supposed to dwell. He concludes that this hazy belief represents a transition from an impersonal religion toward well-defined animism.

There is no doubt that primitive people drew wrong inference from what they saw, as do civilised people today. But there is a vast amount of carefully documented evidence proving that the spirits of the dead return, are seen, and actually communicate with the living. Testimonies state, too, that spirits other than those of human beings which cause material objects to move are in evidence throughout the world.

There is no reason to believe that materialisation, raps, table tipping, poltergeists and similar phenomena are confined to the present day. On the contrary, the evidence indicates that similar kinds of psychic phenomena take place among Aborigines. Thousands of people, many of whom are educated and highly cultured are at the present willing to swear they have been in contact with relatives and friends who have passed on from the physical body.

Fetishism

Here we have the belief that certain material objects, either in their natural state or when prepared according to a special ritual by a priest, have the power of bringing to fulfilment an expectation.

Professor E.W. Hopkins in his book, *History of Religion*, has this to say about the word 'fetish'.

"Many writers use the word loosely to indicate any material object from which, like a mascot, the native expects good luck; but properly a fetish is portable and is unlike a mascot in that it possesses power and will to bless. Hence it is coddled, abused, prayed to and stormed at, exactly as one would treat a recalcitrant spirit who may or may not aid." He also says that a fetish is a spiritual power and does not contain a spirit entity.

It is a common belief that a curse, placed by a person dying a violent death upon some coveted object, has an evil spirit attached to it and will bring bad luck to all who possess it afterwards. Today, of course, we would classify it as a thought force of evil psychokinetic power attached to the object. Some of the Mummies taken from Egyptian tombs have had an uncanny history of tragedy attached to them. These influences, by those who believe in them, are thought to be caused by elemental spirits that were attached to the article by the curses.

A bark painting of ancestral totemic snakes and stringy bark flowers.

In his book, *The Jungle Folk of Africa*, R.H. Milligan, who lived among the Fang tribe of West Africa writes:

"Ancestor worship is the highest form of African fetishism and it is only called fetishism because the ancestor's skull or other part of the body is the medium of communication; the usual fetish of ancestor worship is the skull of the father, which the son keeps in a box. The father occasionally speaks to the son in dreams and frequently communicates with him by omens. He helps him in all his enterprises, good and evil and secures his success in hunting and in war."

While there are elements of both animism and fetishism contained in Totemism it ought to be recognised that the most important religious custom of the Australian Aborigine is Initiation. Without some knowledge of this ceremony Totemism becomes very complex indeed and is almost impossible to understand.

Initiation

An Aboriginal boy cannot attain manhood or a girl marry until he or she has passed the Initiation trials. The ritual fits the Initiate for adult life. The ceremonies of enlightenment vary somewhat between the different tribes but always the rites take them into the deepest mysteries of conviction and faith. During the period of observance, communion with the spirit world plays an important role as do the Laws of Nature and for living a constructive life. Where boys are concerned, the Initiation is quite protracted and very harsh. In some rituals the Initiation is accompanied by circumcision, others require the removal of teeth or some alternative mutilation. The tests endured by girls are less severe than those of the boys and can be acknowledged as rites to celebrate adolescence and preparation for marriage. In either case, the Initiation is important and the trials rigid so that the teachings are firmly implanted in the mind of the recipient.

Among other things, the custom teaches how the Universe was created by an all-pervading Super Intelligence who used the energy associated with the mental power of thought.

Every living entity has a soul which is brought into existence to fulfil a function in the construction, operation and progress of the cosmos toward the Ultimate. The soul never dies, it is something eternal, experiencing good and evil, pain and pleasure through moulding and rejecting forms which it uses as vehicles in the pursuit of knowledge which it must obtain in order to handle more complex situations in the great scheme of things.

There is a continuation of life and personality after the dissolution of the physical body. It is an existence where the human soul personally survives and maintains its familiar characteristics and identity. This invisible, psychic domain can be contacted by proper training in induced emotion and directed thinking. Contact can be made with any living thing by the use of extrasensory perception. Use is made of the hypersensitivity of the nerves to tune in on the psychic or cosmic counterpart of the person, animal, plant or even the environment to be examined. It will be seen how important their religious culture is to the Aborigines; the whole of their lifestyle is subject to supernatural forces and beings which have to be taken into consideration when an examination is made of Totemism.

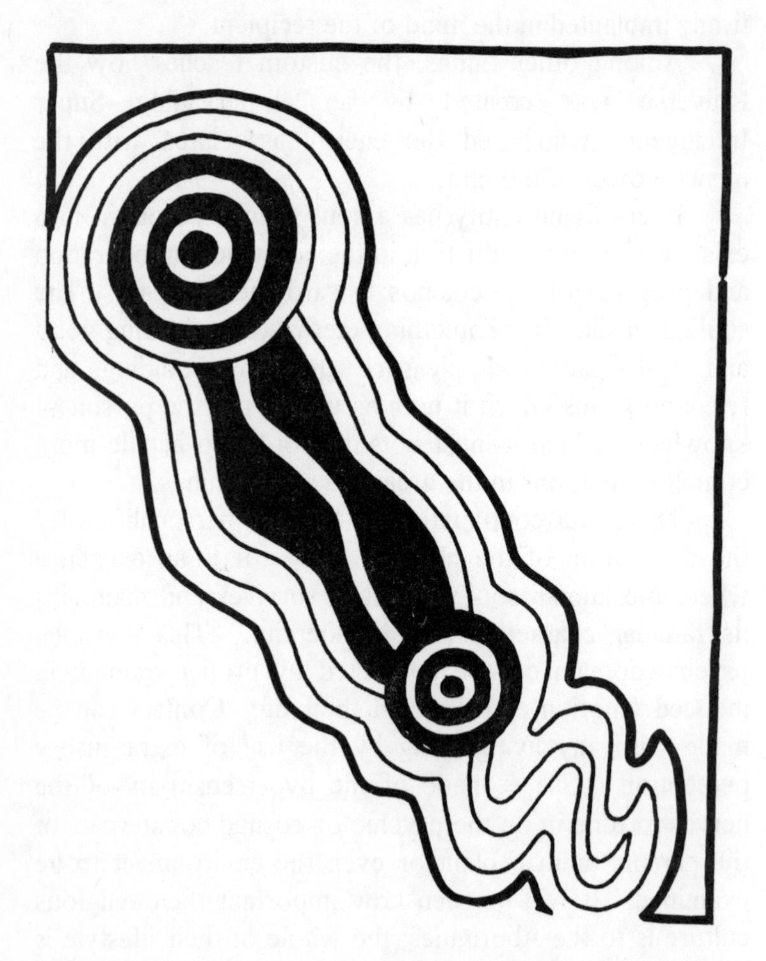

Thalaualla, the black snake. Totem of the Warramunga Tribe.

A totem is a class of material objects which are regarded with superstitious respect by the Aborigine, believing there exists between him and every member of the class an intimate and altogether special relationship. It differs from a fetish in that it embraces an entire class of objects. To the initiated person of the "Black Snake" clan, for example, all black snakes are subject to the same veneration and esteem.

The Aborigine believes that there is a bond of friendship and kinship between the clan of the individual and the totem. Totems may be clan totems, or they may be individual totems. Mutual advantages will result from this relationship, and the totem is actually in some sense the ancestor of the clan or individual to whom it belongs. It is found that a clan or individual expresses the characteristics of its totem. The human group or individual vibrates to the same "key" as that of its totem. The octave is different, but the key is the same, for the totem may be an animal, a plant or some other object. Using astrological terms as an example, the totem is of the same astrological rulership as the person or clan claiming it as a totem.

This natural, sympathetic relationship is used to advantage by the Aborigines. They enter into rapport with the psychic double of the totem. In other words, they use the hypersensitivity of their nerves to tune in on the psychic counterpart of the totem. They do their best to protect and otherwise benefit the totem and in return expect the psychic double to warn them in times of danger, to afford them premonitions of important approaching events and recompense them for their devotions to its welfare. Through their friendship they attempt to use its psychic double to attain advantages for themselves. Although they do not hypnotise their totem, they talk to it, giving it suggestions, much as a hypnotist may suggest to their subject that the latter's psychic body will go to a distant place and obtain certain information or that it directs him or her to a lost article.

Through the natural vibratory resemblance between them, the Aborigine is in rapport with his or her subject or the controlling entity. The totem is a medium controlled by the Aborigines.

To the average Westerner, all this may seem to be nonsense and superstition. Before final judgement is pronounced, however, an investigation ought to be made into just how often a clan is actually warned of danger, probably through extra-sensory perception, by the uncommon actions of some member of its totem.

It might be well to know, for instance, how often a clan in search of game following the direction taken by the first of its totem, actually found abundant game in that direction. Bearing the power of psychokinesis in mind, and how little is know about its technicalities, it might be well to investigate the fortune in tribal welfare of a clan holding a dance in honour of its totem before entering battle, and what effect it had on their endurance, the keenness of their faculties and the impressions by which they took advantage of an opponent, or escaped danger.

Many attempts have been made to classify Totemism into its various categories, but because it is reputed to be regulated by ancestral beings, the whole subject is a complex one which calls for a good deal of correct interp-retation and cannot be detailed here. However, there are some interesting aspects worthy of mention:

1. The spirit of the totem enters the body of the Aboriginal child at the moment of conception. The whole

welfare of the infant depends upon this union and implies that as soon as the soul enters the foetus a spiritual counterpart is formed in the psychic world and is ready for contact and communication.

2. A woman is not authorised to marry a person of the same totemic affiliation. Aboriginal marriage laws are governed by these regulations laid down in the "Dreamtime".

3. Aboriginal people are not permitted to kill or eat an animal which is a member of the same Totemic clan. Totemism is designed to promote a close-knit kinship which works for the welfare of its unit.

4. If a person enters a territory of another tribe he or she is not content until he or she finds someone who shares his or her totem. Having done so, that person can claim kinship and safety whilst visiting or passing through that land.

5. There is a very strong link between the human and superhuman dimensions of existence. The totem symbolises the bond between the two worlds and is expressed by a sacred design generally drawn, carved or shaped on to some selected object.

Totemism has had a very large influence on aboriginal art. Indeed, most paintings, carvings, the dress used at corroborees and sacred ceremonies, are representative of the totems and the ancestral beings who create them. A personal totem is a most precious possession, a reason for living, a source of identification, a "key" to the spirit world and a passport through life. The Aboriginal Wisemen ~ by the use of Totemic Laws ~ are as qualified to resolve problems as modern day lawyers. They are, in fact, the "constitution" of the Aboriginal way of life. It is impossible to go into the intricacies of all the different orders of observance, but the efficiency of the Laws of Totemism in controlling a community is amazing.

Totemism, in essence, means a spiritual link between a particular environment, plant, animal or mineral and an unborn child which binds a person-in-the-making to the totem forever. It is, broadly, a kinship of people and Nature which operates not only here in the physical world but in the spiritual life beyond. A doctrine of universal kinship and welfare in which communication is made through the use of extra-sensory perception. In the Aboriginal world this predetermines a great deal of its future and behaviour.

The confiscation of land rights by the white people ignorant of Totemism has deprived an Aboriginal community of the whole of its spiritual support. It has lost all immediate purpose, and since its constitution can no longer operate, the people disperse, dwindle and are forced to accept whatever is in store for them. The decay of Totemism is responsible for the frustrations and feelings of hopelessness amongst the Australian Aborigines today.

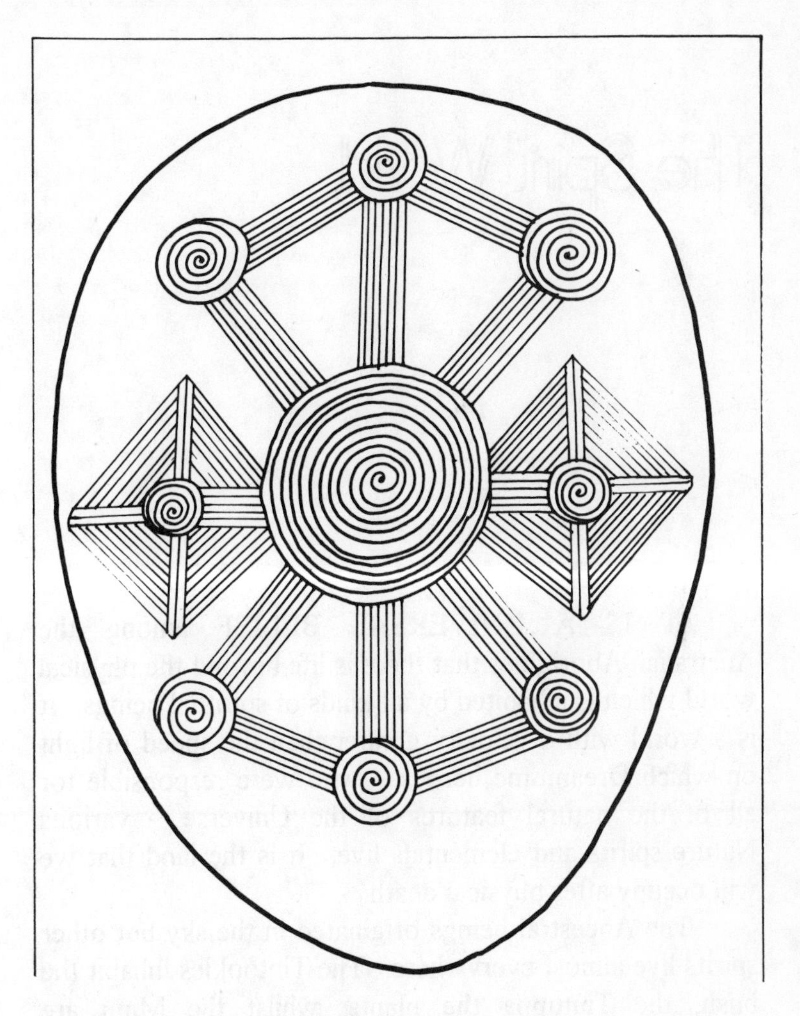

A sacred stone from Central Australia. The carvings represent the journeys of the ancestral beings in the spirit world who were later to become totems.

The Spirit World

IT IS A UNIVERSAL BELIEF among the Australian Aborigines that there is life beyond the physical world which is inhabited by all kinds of spiritual beings. It is a world with a velocity greater than the speed of light on which Dreamtime heroes ~ who were responsible for all of the natural features of the Universe ~ various Nature spirits and elementals live. It is the land that we will occupy after physical death.

The Ancestral beings originated in the sky but other spirits live almost everywhere. The Tintookies inhabit the bush, the Tintuppa the plants, whilst the Mimi are generally found among the rocks. While there is no uniformity of belief, there is no doubt that these forces are recognised as an essential element to continuing life. Death is not the end, but a transition from one state of life to another. There is abundant and convincing proof explaining that there is a realm in which human souls survive after death. Further evidence indicates that when they pass to this region their familiar characteristics and identities are maintained. But up to the present time, all information concerning the environments of that land and the activities of those surviving them, comes to most people as hearsay evidence and consequently cannot be considered as incontrovertible proof.

The Australian Aboriginal version then, given by the learned Wirinun or Shaman, is of interest to all students of comparative religions and the Ancient Wisdom.

The Wirinun receives special training in extra-sensory perception and the extension of his consciousness on to the Dowie, astral and spiritual dimension during Initiation. A qualified Shaman must have experienced a ritual death, followed by transformation in order to heighten sensitivity to psychic influences. During the exercise of extended consciousness, the electromagnetic energy is largely withdrawn from the physical body and converted into energies with a velocity greater than that of light. It is used to sustain the completely withdrawn Dowie, or astral body, in its journey to the spiritual dimension. In this state, only a single elastic astral thread connects the individual with their physical body.

By using the process, the Wirinun is able to visit, in person, the realms of those who have passed on from the physical world. It is a direct link between the daily life and the Dreamtime, something essential for the well-being of the tribe. He is able to talk with departed loved ones, meet the Ancestral beings and bring back fresh evidence of the laws to be followed in order to meet the environment of the day.

Mimi. Elemental spirits, most of which are elongated in appearance, as seen by clairvoyant painters.

Another common method of contacting the spirit world is by the use of the hypersensitivity of the nerves to tune in on the Dowie or astral counterparts of the spiritual person or environment to be examined. The nervous system, or some part of it, becomes a receiving set through which the electrical energies and astral forces closely associated with it pick up ~ radio fashion ~ the subtle vibrations radiated by whatever it is tuned to. The individual will then feel the condition which they have contacted. By the use of these methods, the Wirinun can give convincing evidence of the conditions in the spiritual world. But to the world at large, these experiences are only credible to the extent to which faith is placed in the authenticity and veracity of the narrator. There are, of course, numerous Aborigines, particularly amongst the older people, who naturally or by cultivating it, have their soul-sense so active that they are able, without leaving the physical body, to see, hear, taste, feel and smell the things of the subtler realms.

The science of the spirit world is important to the Aborigines. They want to know details of the great plan for life mapped out by Baiame, the Creator, and the Ancestral beings. The entities of the Dowie can give them information concerning the past, present and future, which will enable them to direct their efforts towards something broader than just the sojourn here on Tya, the Earth.

Contact with the Next Life

The great difficulty in explaining and describing life after death lies in the fact that due to the velocities of that region, there is a different order of distance, time and gravitation. That is, ordinary time, distance and gravitation do not exist. The Wirinun makes it quite clear that this is why to us, here on the Earth, the spiritual Dowie seems to be full of contradictions. When objects attain velocities greater than 186,284 miles per second ~ the speed of light ~ they lose all of their physical properties and gain the characteristics of the spiritual world. They are not different objects in the sense that they have lost their identities, rather, they have lost certain physical properties but have gained others.

Because a man loses weight, purchases new clothes and learns to speak another language does not mean that he has lost his identity. He has lost one quality and gained another; he is, nevertheless, the same man. So it is that when an object or a person loses the physical body, new propensities are made available, but the identity remains. The physical properties with which we are familiar, such as weight and temperature, are made possible by the low velocities of physical things.

According to the Wirinun, there are seven levels of vibratory frequencies on the Dowie. The relationship between these levels or regions is vertical in Nature, one being above the other, not in three-dimensional space but in vibratory rate. By withdrawing much of the electro-magnetic energy from his body and converting it into the higher velocity Dowie energies, he is able to move out of his physical body and by adjusting the vibratory rates of his Dowie to this region, he is instantly in this realm and taking part in its happenings.

He can move about and communicate at will. It is a complete world and so long as he holds the vibratory rate firmly, he can remain there.

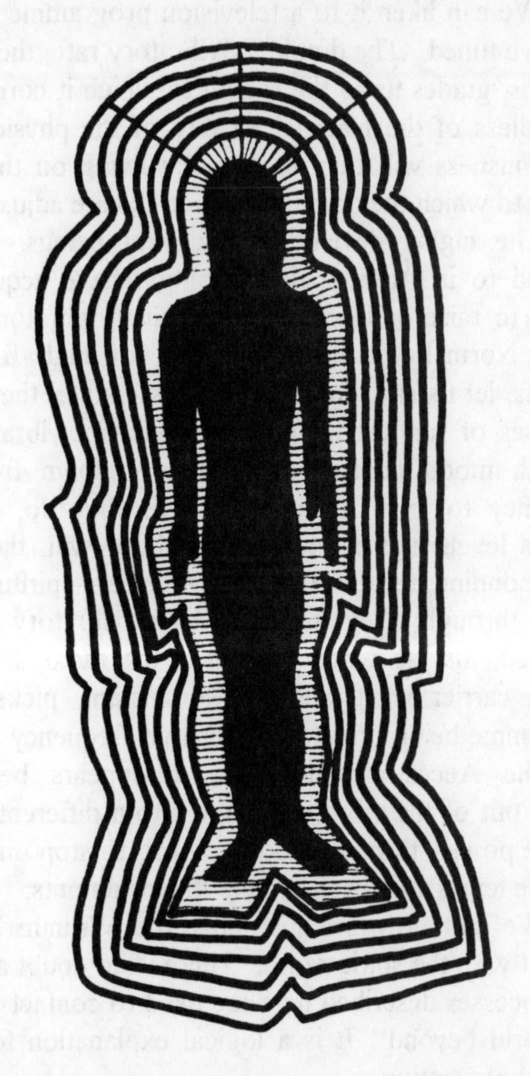

In the centre is the physical body. Surrounding the physical body is the Mullowill. Outside of the Mullowill are the seven vibratory divisions of the Dowie.

We can liken it to a television programme to which we have tuned. The dominant vibratory rate, the Wirinun explains, guides us to the region to which it corresponds. Regardless of the material locality of the physical body, consciousness will then be actually living on the Dowie region to which the dominant vibrations are adjusted.

The highly developed Ancestral beings, so often referred to in Aboriginal mythology, have acquired the power to raise or lower their dominant vibratory rate at will. Normally living on a level of high frequency, perhaps, let us say, the seventh Dowie state, they do, for purposes of service, lower their dominant vibratory rate through mood control. They slow down from high frequency to low frequency and as they do, pass the various levels and enter successively at will, the worlds corresponding to these levels. As this spiritual being moves through a region with a basic vibratory rate it is glimpsed, just as when one turns the radio dial past a certain carrier wave and, for an instant, picks up the programme being broadcast over that frequency. So it is that the Ancestral spirit-being disappears because it moves out of the vibratory range into a different one. It has the power, through mood control, to stop on any one of these levels and teach or help the inhabitants.

We can now see just how the Wirinun keeps in rapport with the spirit world. There is no doubt at all that the processes described here are used to contact all life in the world beyond. It is a logical explanation for extra-sensory perception.

Life in the Spiritual World

Conscious life, according to the Wirinun, exists on every vibratory level or region of the Dowie dimension. On the lower levels the forms and processes are similar in detail to those of the life forms here on Tya, the Earth, yet even those on these lower strata have properties they do not possess on Earth. People, for example, walk without moving their feet. When they concentrate on a particular environment, they move as though being swept into it. The lower levels of the Dowie dimension have a basic vibratory rate close to those common to the physical world. The Dowie dimension, however, is thought built. Thought communion is as common a property to the Dowie as vocal communion is here on Earth. To think a thing intently is to build it up out of subtle substance.

Here on Earth, the Wirinun explains, the white person thinks a house, then builds it physically by placing each piece of material in its proper place until the final result is achieved. But after death, the same house can be built by thought, provided we learn how to use our thoughts, because of the plasticity of Dowie substance to thought power. All we have to do is to visualise such a house and bring it into existence in all of its detail.

Thought power is emphasised in all Aboriginal Initiation Ceremonies and is practised continuously in faith healing, rain-making, the pointing of the bone and all of the so-called Magic of the Wirinun. It is, he expounds, something which ought to be studied carefully by every person on Tya, for it is the most powerful force in the Universe and the answer to all future progression.

When called upon to explain the most striking difference between the physical world and the next life, the Wirinun will unhesitatingly tell you that the most forceful impression is the immediate response to thought. On each of the regions of the Dowie or near to Tya, the scenery is much the same. There are mountains, trees, flowers, birds and so on just as we find them here. But the colours are more brilliant and intense. The notes of the singing birds are very much clearer and have beauty of tone. On the higher regions the vegetation is even brighter and the creatures there are of higher intelligence, with greater spiritual affinity than those who perform similar functions here on Tya.

The next dimension is not, according to the Wirinun, some weird strange place. With a few improvements, life there is much as it is here on Tya. People think much more clearly and comprehensively, feel more intently, and act with greater speed. They know more and do more without suffering fatigue. In every way it is a progressed form of our life.

Those who love us will still love us, and those who opposed us here on Tya ~ unless they have gained in wisdom ~ will still have a tendency to oppose us. But if they belong to a different vibratory level than we, they will be unable to affect us. In any event, if we are to advance in this realm, we will compose and adjust our differences in the work for a more important cause. Loved ones also may occupy a different vibratory level, but if the love is strong and persistent it finds a way for the one above to visit and encourage the one below. The one below can build a character which will enable him or her to move to a higher level.

In matters of injury to others, it takes time, conferences and the advice of wise teachers like the Wirinun who have advanced to higher levels of the spiritual realms, to find a way to solve problems. Here on Tya, each Aboriginal tribe has a Council of Elders, composed of the Shaman or Wirinun, Great Hunters and Ceremonial Leaders, a Council which is neither judge or jury, but takes part in the functions of both. The Council of Elders is, presumably, similar in structure to that of the spirit world.

Other ties of Tya also carry responsibilities into the next life. Those we contact and influence here may present a debt that calls for readjustment. We may feel that the best way to right a wrong is to do something helpful for the same individual in the after-life. So that we may feel at ease, it is necessary to pay our debts. The record of our lives is before us and we act as both judge and jury.

Money has no power to buy anything in the regions of the spirit world that one visits. Possessions have no real purchasing power whatsoever. The difference is not that there is payment, for the currency is different, it is one of constructive service. The individual of the next dimension who renders service receives nothing and wants nothing.

Here on Tya, the original black Australians used an exchange system of gifts between adjacent tribes enabling them to share their resources. "Bush" tribes provide herbs, game and honey in exchange for fish from the coastal clans. The receiver of a gift is never under obligation to the donor but as personal and tribal prestige is involved it is important that the recipient returns a gift of greater value than that received. The system is of great benefit to all of the participants and, here again, is believed to be based on the spiritual teachings of the Dreamtime. It emphasises the importance of training, whilst here on Tya, of overcoming selfishness and greed which have no place in the spiritual world.

But there are regions, apparently, in the Dowie where money of some kind does exist. It is found only in the lower realms where the miserly and greedy gravitate, the malignant spirits of Aboriginal Philosophy. Even at the time of the earliest creations on Tya, Baiame, the great spirit and the Ancestral beings had to battle against the forces of evil. The legend of flowers and the plague of insects are typical examples.

The "Plague of Insects" is worth noting and is explained by the Wirinun who recalls how Baiame, having fashioned the geography of Tya, then covered it with all kinds of vegetation. It was a beautiful sight as millions of all kinds of plants tossed to and fro with joy. But Marmoo, the spirit of evil from the lower realms of the Dowie, was jealous of the charm and elegance of the great spirit's works and set out to spoil the plant life.

In secrecy, he produced a tribe of insects, creatures that would fly, crawl and burrow, to destroy the world of earthly vegetation. The devouring swarms ate the leaves of trees, the grass and everything else before them. Tya grew bare and ugly as the ravenous hoards swarmed over the mountains and plains. With the aid of Nungeena, the esteemed Spirit of Nature, the lyre and other birds were produced to rid the world of destruction.

So long as we, then, in the physical world, are unable to perceive the value of motives other than jealousy, greed and profit, we are chained by our own desires to the lower spiritual realms where people fight and struggle among themselves, in what can be termed the spiritual hells of the next life. The only "currency", recommends the Wirinun, that will help after physical death is to see what can be done to benefit others.

The esoteric student will be pleased to learn that, according to the Wirinun, those genuinely interested in the subject will be able to attend, rather than visit, through "astral travel" while in the physical form, schools which deal with all aspects of the Forces of Nature. The work of the bark painter, or artist, whatever the medium, is only partly expressed in the physical creations of his music, painting, dancing or whatever he uses to give form to his work. The important thing to him and to others is the direct way in which he conveys through the sense of beauty to the very interior nature of others.

Operating with high velocities, through the avenue of thought forms, he imparts to others and cultivates in them his own joyous appreciation of the symmetrical, the harmonious, the beautiful and all that seems the most elevating in life.

The spiritual world of the Aborigines is an exciting place. It is a life that is brilliant and pleasingly active, where interests are varied and thrilling and there is more real romance than has even been thought of on Tya. Social relations are given plenty of attention. Amusements and entertainment, instead of being considered a waste of time are deemed important in every well-regulated life. Life, after the physical death, it seems, is going to be intensely more alluring, happy and vital provided we have high and noble aspirations which will provide energy that will take us to higher levels than the purgatorial regions which has the vibrations of the brute, the deceitful, jealous and selfish.

The Tijuringa, or sacred boards and objects, the Gayandi or Bullroarer, the Bora grounds, Initiation,

Totemism, Ritual and Ceremony are all proof of the emphasis placed on the spiritual world by the Aborigines. Is it any wonder that they are so conversant with the next life?

"Illa Booker Mer Ley Urrie Urrie - The Soul Will Not Die!"

The Universe, as we know it, moves largely through mechanical principles. But behind these principles and behind the arrangement of the various physical and spiritual worlds is intelligent direction and guidance. The spirit world of the Aborigines is a part of the controlling force.

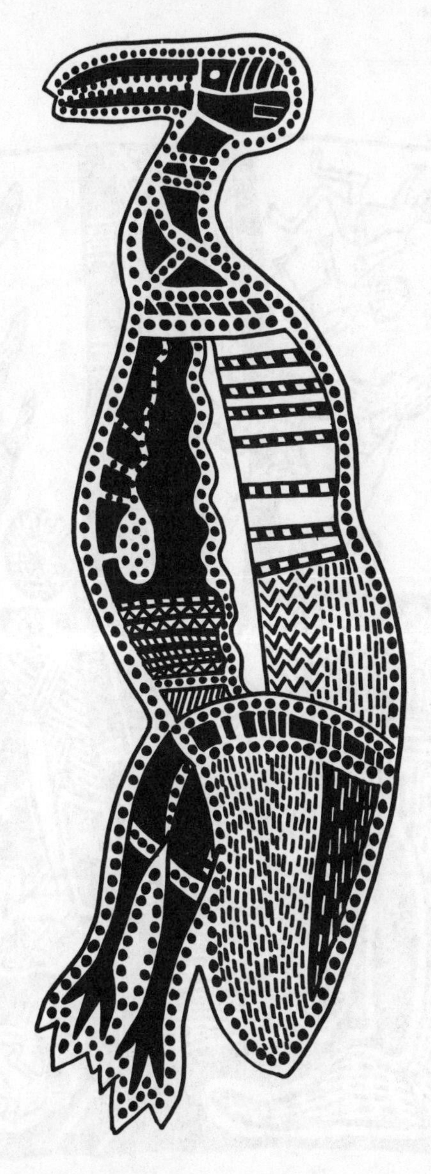

X-ray painting of native companion or jabiru.

A bark painting depicting the death of an Aboriginal man and his journey to the spirit world.

Top Left: The spirit body leaves the decaying physical body lying on the funeral platform.
Bottom Left: The didgeridoo player and dancers performing sacred death rites.
Top Right: The spirit of the man and dancers' spirit bodies perform the ritual which ensures a safe journey.
Bottom Right: The spirit body of the dead man kills a fish with a stone. This will be his food during the journey to the spirit world where he will take his rightful place.

Bark Painting and Rock Carving

ANTHROPOLOGISTS REPORT THAT ABORIGINAL BARK PAINTING began when tribespeople, forced to take refuge from wet weather, decorated the inside of their bark shelters by painting them with designs and symbols depicting life in the area from a legend from the past.

Bark shelters, known as wirlies, are made of a basic frame of tree branches to which are attached long strips of bark taken from the bush. There is no doubt that they gave the Aborigine, interested in painting and with time to spare, an incentive to do something about decorating the dull interior of the shelter.

While the view of the anthropologist is logical, there is no doubt that bark paintings and rock carvings were used to convey an accumulation of knowledge gained over a long period of time. It would seem that crude pictographs carved into rock by the original Australians sought to make permanent records, convey ideas and refresh memories of happenings of tribal importance. Gradually, as a form of progression, they developed into coloured bark paintings which were easier to handle and interpret.

The process of bark painting aided the black people tremendously in their acquisition of knowledge, they were no longer dependent upon a tribe member's memory to give them access to information based upon the experiences of generations of the past. The bark paintings are records of the Dreamtime.

The Shaman of Aboriginal tribes realised that knowledge was essential for all further progress towards greater nutrition, benefits for their off-spring and significance through more ample expression relative to life on Earth and the spiritual world beyond. Their only hope of improving their condition was through increasing and using the knowledge of these two environments and the laws operating in each of them.

To increase knowledge, not only must the experiences of people be collected, analysed and given sound interpretation, but there must always be additional research. This principle applied to both dimensions of existence, for the Shaman realised the desire to find expression for the three irrepressible drives of nutrition, reproduction and significance, not merely during a person's physical life but also later when their work on Earth is done.

In addition, if people were to benefit by his knowledge, then they must have ready access to it. This meant that ways had to be devised by which those responsible for administrating the Laws of the Dreamtime could not suppress or distort the facts. They were not meant to remain static, but to develop and progress indefinitely. So it was that the rock carvings began to appear, followed by a more sophisticated form on bark at a later date.

While experience and extra-sensory perception taught the Shaman how to solve the problems with which he was faced, frequently the only avenue of existence in a harsh and changing environment was through adaptation and use of knowledge. The carvings and paintings showed where game could be found, advised on where to locate water and totemic sites, and provided a host of information dealing with the necessities required for survival.

The Aborigines have always used art as a bond between themselves and the spiritual world. Now, of course, it is being commercialised and all kinds of supposed original works are being produced and are obtainable from almost anywhere. Regrettably, it is but another phase in the destruction of Aboriginal culture. A deeply religious people, the Aborigines suffer a severe emotional loss when their culture is suppressed. Every effort should be made to utilise the talents of the Australian black person. It may be necessary to introduce them to new materials and media through which they can make a most worthwhile contribution to modern civilisation.

How Bark is Painted

There is little refinement in the materials used for bark painting for they are all secured from the natural bush-land. The exercise begins by selecting a suitable stringy bark tree. The branches are chosen from those well up the trunk so that the piece used for the painting will be free of knots. Blemishes such as those caused by termites, borers and other insects which can affect the surface are carefully checked. By using a sharp axe or hatchet, two cuts are inserted around the tree; the first, twelve or eighteen inches from the bottom and a second, as required to complete the size of the bark for painting. The two incisions are then joined by a vertical cut and the sheet is ready to remove. The edges of the vertical split are turned back and pressure is applied to remove the bark which being green and moist, falls away easily without breaking. The trimming is then done in order to remove all but the innermost layer and the sheet is ready for curing by fire and heat.

The bark is placed on a bed of dry leaves. Twigs and grass are spread evenly over these and they are set alight so that the warmth will remove all excess moisture. It is heated on both sides so that any excess bark burns away, making it easier to remove when final trimming begins. The sheet is then taken from the smouldering mound and trodden down on to the ground and pinned with heavy stones to keep it from twisting and buckling. It will take four or five days to season. When the sheet is declared dry it is given its final trim and shaped ready for use. A good bark painting ought to be fitted with stretchers, which are two straight sticks bound firmly across either end to prevent warping. Too many good bark paintings have been ruined because this process has been forgotten.

The palette of the painter is usually dictated by the materials available. It is generally restricted to four basic pigments of black, white, red and yellow. The reds shade into browns and the yellows come from the ochre derived from oxides, haematite, limonite and so on. White generally comes from pipe clay, black from charcoal. The materials are ground finely between stones and mixed with fixatives such as honey, the yolk of bird's eggs or the juice of native lily bulbs and water. Each painter has a variety of brushes which are sometimes two-ended and made from hair, feathers, leaf fibres bound together at one end or sticks which are frayed at the ends.

The artist does not use an easel, but places the sheet of bark on the ground or across his knees. He either walks around the bark when painting or turns it around in front of him. It is necessary to understand this procedure because to "read" a bark painting it should be viewed from above, for that is how the painter sees his work in production. Bark paintings are not to be hung on the wall.

The artist is not limited to a standard procedure; he is free to follow his own methods. There is never a division between painters and non-painters, every person is a potential artist. The only restriction comes when sacred symbols, designs and work, making reference to the Dreamtime, is required. These paintings are done in secret and sometimes the painting is accompanied by chanting of the artist or other tribal members, so that the artist is in rapport with the situation he is to portray.

They are stored in hidden places and revealed only at the progressive levels of initiation. Their use is paralleled by that of other forms of artistic expression ~ totemic paintings on the body and on other objects such as stones, wood carvings and so on. The sacred works link the artist and those who view his paintings with the supernatural powers of the Alcheringa and spiritual world.

There are periods, of course, when the artist deals with the events of every day life. The kangaroos, wallabies, lizards and snakes of the bush are a common theme of the inland communities while fishing scenes predominate in the coastal areas. Probably the most interesting of all bark paintings are found in the X-ray form of art which feature the body of a subject from both the external and internal view. It is a method of explaining that there is much more to a body than its outward appearance.

Following on from the X-ray art there is the work which involves itself with the Nature spirits, entities and elements of the world beyond. These painters, in the main, claim to be clairvoyant and are able to see and describe life on that dimension of existence. They are depicted in all kinds of situations both good and bad. European influence is now making itself felt and as the environment for the Aborigines changes, so does their art. It is now quite common to see landscapes with topography arranged in perspective which is foreign to the style used in the original barks and rocks.

In sacred painting, however, there is a strict adherence to the Law of the Dreamtime. The Wirinun and Tribal Elders see that the message is retained exactly as it had been passed on down through the ages. The original text must be preserved at all costs so that the teachings can be applied to the environment of the day through correct interpretation by those best equipped to do so. These are the permanent records passed down from generation to generation.

The First Bark Paintings

Although the first decorated barks are reported to have been found in Tasmania in 1807, when the French explorers Peron and Freyeiret visited that country, crude pictures were seen on rocks long before that time. Many examples are still in a state of good preservation. Obviously the bark painting is an extension of the carvings on rock. The earliest accounts of the paintings reveal that they were used in conjunction with the sacred ceremonies of the Alcheringa. Large sheets of bark covered with elaborate designs of symbolism were displayed on the trees and poles in conjunction with the important initiation rituals.

Personally, I have always considered the paintings of Northern Australia superior in character to anywhere else. They are rich in colour and design and have an eye appeal of outstanding quality. Even today, they have a deep ritual significance in the sacred ceremonies of the Bora lands in that region. On the other hand, in the centre of Australia, where there is a lack of suitable materials, bark painting seems to have lost its significance so far as being important to ritual ceremony. In the South, most of the Bora grounds have been destroyed so that any kind of painting is rare.

Interest by white people is gaining in momentum, both in the art itself and its expression of social, religious and economic life of the original Australians. This is a most promising state of affairs for Aboriginal welfare and indeed for the furthering of universal kinship.

It ought be remembered that in true pictograph it is very difficult to convey abstract ideas of any kind. Its use is therefore quite limited. But where there is also a spoken language, it is but a step, though a long step and an exceedingly important one to unite the picture of the object as a representation of the more general conception. 'Be' and 'bee' or 'not' and 'knot' are identical. It is impossible to draw a picture of the general conception of 'not' and 'be'. It is very easy to depict in pictograph a bee in flight or a knot in a rope. This picture, then, because the words sound the same, becomes the symbol of 'be' as well as 'bee' and 'not' as well as 'knot'. The picture is a phonetic sign.

Just as the ancient Egyptians used phonetic signs in writing, so do the Aborigines use them in bark paintings, particularly where sacred work is concerned. The average white person finds them difficult to understand. One asks, did the Australian Aborigine derive the general idea from the same source as the ancient Egyptians who used pictures called hieroglyphics?

Bark painting like many other aspects of Aboriginal culture is worthy of further investigation. Its history has all the intrigue and fascination of other painting stories of the world.

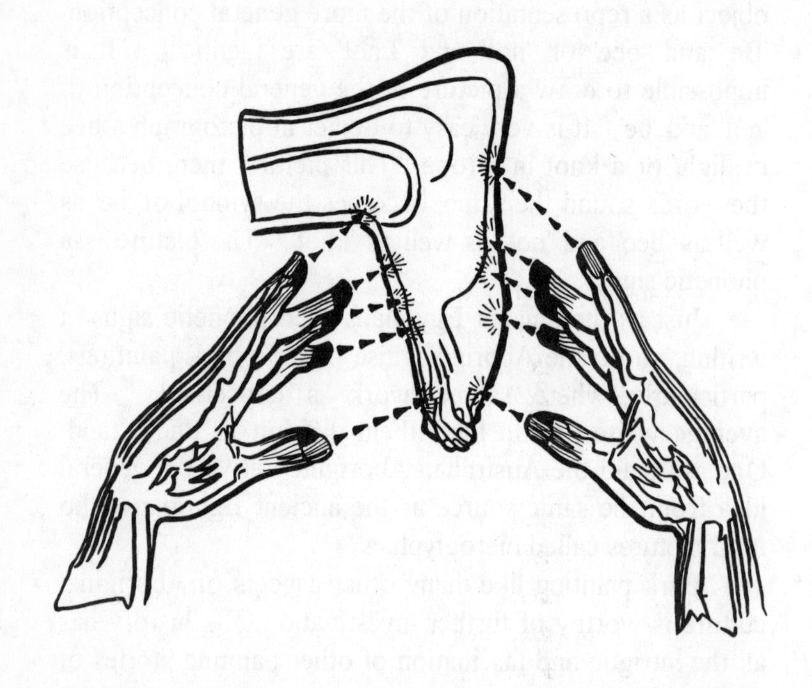

Aboriginal laying on of hands. The electromagnetic or tumpinyeri mooroop energy passing through healing hands.

Natural Healing

THE ABORIGINAL WIRINUN OR SHAMAN has been described as a phoney by many white people when it comes to the healing of the sick. He is reported to use sleight of hand, trickery, fear and potions to rid members of his tribe from sickness. These treatments are claimed to be fake and of no consequence.

The Aborigines, like most other people, use domestic remedies for simple, everyday complaints. Herbs taken from the bush-land are used for internal disorders, heat is administered for pain and bone fractures are treated by setting them in mud plaster and supporting them with firm binding. It is interesting, however, to study the practice of faith healing used by the Wirinun to prevent and cure the many illnesses which lay beyond the scope of the ordinary person.

In a world peopled by spirits with super-human powers and a Wirinun, with so-called magical attributes, able to contact the spiritual world and utilise the Laws of Nature at will, is it any wonder that great faith is placed in the expertise of this revered man?

The Wirinun undergoes extensive training in both faith healing and the laying on of hands. He is instructed by an accepted practitioner, experiences a symbolic death, a visit to the spirit world, goes through a period of isolation and meditation. He studies diet, herbs, the hidden powers of Nature, and in particular, the importance of electromagnetic energy, or *Tumpinyeri Mooroop,* the Life Spirit. The preparation for the work is almost exclusively spiritual, similar to that of the yogi or monk, rather than that of a medical practitioner, as we know them. It is training that is relevant to the Aboriginal world.

The practice of healing, the Wirinun explains, emphasises faith and proper rapport between the patient and the healer. In other words, the sick person must believe that he or she will be cured. There are those amongst the Wirinun who are natural healers and others who develop the ability mainly through communicating energies to the patient through the hands which are held close to, or actually in contact with, the part to be healed.

This method of healing was used by Jesus, who instructed his twelve disciples in the art. In turn, the method was entrusted to those who followed in his footsteps. Because the healing energies are more easily imparted to the patient through the healer's fingers, Christians who use it commonly refer to it as "healing by laying on of hands".

Mixing herbs for medicinal purposes in a coolamon (wooden bowl).

"Then he called his twelve disciples together and gave the power and authority over all devils and to cure diseases and sent them to preach the Kingdom of God and to heal the sick". (Luke 9:1,2).

If we are to believe the New Testament, the two things which Jesus commanded his followers to do and emphasised in a manner to indicate they were of equal importance, were to preach the Gospel and heal the sick. Historians record that healing was a common practice among all believers in Christianity for several hundred years after the Crucifixion. Iransus Chronicles, 110: "Man healed the sick by laying their hands on them."

I present no brief favouring Christianity, but I am pointing out to those who follow this religion that its founder placed equal emphasis on preaching and healing by laying on of hands. It is to be presumed that a leader who knew he was departing from Earth would embody in his last command to those who were to carry on his work that which he considered most important. Jesus indicated how those who were true Christians might be known from those who were merely pretenders to Christianity:

"These signs shall follow them that believe: In my name . . . they shall lay hands on the sick and they shall recover." Religion and healing went hand in hand in those times.

The Australian Aborigines have always recognised the teaching of the great spirit Baiame, which is similar to that of Jesus. Baiame manifested into the form of a man sometime after the Great Flood and was the first Shaman to teach the techniques of healing.

It is the function of religion, surely, not merely to teach people how best to live, but also to help them to live in a manner which contributes most to universal welfare. The Wirinun explains that an individual cannot contribute his utmost to the welfare of the tribe when ill, so that a knowledge of healing is necessary in order to help him regain his health.

It is not necessary for the Aboriginal Medicinemen, who cured by laying on of hands, to know that some of the energy which passed through their bodies and out of their hands was electromagnetic and that it was derived from energy drawn from the Universe. For them to benefit from sunshine did not mean that it was necessary for them to know the nature of Light, for even today, modern science does not really know whether it is a wave or corpuscular, or both.

They learned by experience how to get warm in the sunshine and they are taught the technique of tuning in on an energy from the Universe and permit it to pass through their bodies as a healing current. Even Akhenaten of Egypt, who taught and practised this healing technique more than 1,300 years before the twelve disciples were born, probably had no notion of tuning in on the energy he desired to use. How such energies are picked up by the nervous system, acting as a radio receiver, is knowledge made possible only since the discovery of the radio. But Akhenaten, the twelve disciples and the Aboriginal Wirinun, through actual practice, learned how healing energies from some source outside themselves were induced to flow through their bodies and into the bodies of others to produce healing.

The Wirinun healers tune in, in a way similar to how we tune in to a radio set, to the vibratory rate of the energy they desire and then direct the flow through the finger tips to the part or organ to be healed. It would seem that there are three distinct types of energy:

a) The electromagnetic energy of the healer which passes from his hands to the patient.

b) The thoughts and mental images in the healer's mind which call up and direct the electromagnetic energies to the accomplishment of the specific healing work in hand.

c) Contact with the Dowie, or Spiritual World, which enables the healer to call for assistance from entities of that sphere experienced in the healing process and able, because of their x-ray vision, to pin-point the cause of the disease.

While it is the *Tumpinyeri Mooroop* or electromagnetic energy which more directly brings about changes in the physical body, the changes are determined by the Dowie energies which guide them in their task. Other than being the energy of life, electromagnetic energy itself accomplishes very little. It is plastic, takes direction and does such work as the Dowie energies direct. When imparted through the hands to a patient with the thought of benefiting them, it gives vitality and strength. It can also be directed to destroy or bring about changes in the tissue. In so far as it can communicate its motions to physical substance, it tends to reproduce in matter whatever form or condition is present in the astral substance with which it is associated.

The physical structure can only be changed through the action of electromagnetic energy. Therefore it is essential that there is sufficient electromagnetic energy present to bring about the desired change. As it is the Life of the body, this energy needs to be present in ample amounts. No matter how perfect the physique, if the *Tumpinyeri Mooroop* or electromagnetic energy becomes depleted, Life departs. So far as the physical body is concerned, it is the vital fluid and because it is so important, an organ having an abundance of it will tend to be healthy and able to throw off disease.

Electromagnetism normally passes from the hands of a healer. The energies flowing from the right hand of a right-handed person are electric and tend to concentrate the nerve currents of the patient's body in the region of the healer's hand. The energies flowing from the left hand are magnetic and tend to diffuse the nerve currents of the patient's body in that part of the healer's hand. Commonly, if the healer is left-handed the reverse is true.

The nerve currents of the body are electromagnetic and influence the flow of the blood. Blood tends to flow more abundantly to any region where there is nerve stimulation or the concentration of nervous energy. Consequently, adding the electric energy of the right hand to a part, tends to give it not merely a healing energy but also an additional blood supply. This may be what the tissue needs.

On the other hand, if the condition to be cured is due to congestion, it needs to be relaxed. The nerve currents are flowing too freely to the affected part and the unusual blood supply tends to increase the inflammation, perhaps even robbing other parts of the body. When such condition exists, instead of positive electric energy, what is needed is the soothing, relaxing, pacifying magnetic energy from the left hand. That is, what the tissues or organs need is not more vitality but more of the healing, soothing, feminine energy of the magnetic constitution.

In using electromagnetic energies, when the Wirinun wishes to cause a boil to come to a head, or the poisons of the body to be collected in a certain spot, he places his right hand directly over the inflamed part and his left hand is as nearly directly opposite as possible. Whenever there is any inflammation which tends to produce pus, the right hand is placed directly over it causing a drawing sensation. When there is an old sore which needs a new blood supply, the right hand is placed over the sore and the left hand opposite.

When the Wirinun wishes to diffuse the poison and scatter it, he places his left hand over the inflamed part and the right hand on the opposite side of the limb or body. The magnetism from the left hand is of opposite polarity tending to soothe rather than stimulate. It relaxes the part and scatters the poison along with the blood from the spot.

To quote an example, if the liver is afflicted, the Wirinun's right hand is placed over the liver and the left hand placed on the back opposite. This may cause pain but if his hands are reversed, the pain ceases. Often a diseased part which is made worse through electro-magnetic forces from one hand is healed by the electromagnetism from the other hand. That is, according to the special need of the part to be healed, both positive electricity and negative magnetism have healing properties.

Electromagnetic energy or *Tumpinyeri Mooroop* does not flow easily from cold fingers ~ coldness indicates that they have a poor blood supply. Therefore, before treatment, the hands are rubbed together, the arms flung about vigorously so as to ensure that they are not only warm, but pulsating with the blood that has been forced into them. Another consideration put forward by the Wirinun is that *Tumpinyeri Mooroop*, or electromagnetic energy, does not flow very well from dry fingers. If the fingers are dry, even if warm and full of blood, it indicates that the electromagnetic energy is not flowing from them properly for treatment. When they are warm and slightly damp with perspiration, they are in the best condition to give treatment.

The most important function of healing is not so much to cure the sick, but to keep people well. The Wirinun admits that we must cure disease, but to him it is far more important to keep the disease from manifesting. Instead of bragging about his cures, he will feel ashamed when members of the tribe fall ill.

The thoughts of the Wirinun are always directed towards the earnest desire to return his patient to health. The desires of the thought cells can be changed in the direction sought through conversion. He instructs the patient in the constructive use of thoughts and he employs the same positive course in giving a specific treatment. It is always delivered with pleasure and the earnestness that they will cure. The thoughts may take a wide variety of forms. If there is a hindrance in objective consciousness to recognise the true desires, the Wirinun will get the confidence of his patient sufficiently so, that he will talk about him or herself freely and reveal these habitual thought trends. When the trends that express the inner discord are discovered, the Wirinun will instruct the patient to substitute pleasant thoughts of the antidote type so as to remove those that were previously habitual and perhaps harmful. In other words, discordant thoughts about work, illness and anything else that promotes fear must be removed from the patient.

All physical cells and organs have a certain amount of intelligence, according to the Wirinun. They know how to do certain things and if their consciousness can be reached and impressed by the Wirinun they will strive to do as he instructs. Baiame, the Super Intelligence of the Aboriginal people, is said to have implanted a portion of his power into every living thing, and intelligence grows as the result of experience through pain and pleasure. The same principle applies to the cells of the physical body. Their consciousness, as well as the unconscious mind of the patient, resides on the Dowie, or spiritual dimension. They can be reached and impressed through the organic electromagnetic energy of the Wirinun acting as a conductor of his thoughts.

The power of suggestion and thought power so frequently used by the Aborigines is here used to advantage. By so doing, he expresses himself to his patient in words and actions that he or she will be healed. It is a question of the active gaining control over the passive.

Throughout the whole of the treatment, the Wirinun will hold in his mind the image of his patient in perfect health, not only objectively, but also with his spiritual self. He is determined that the patient shall and must gain the health he desires. When he knows that it will be beneficial for some group of physical cells or some organ to behave in a different manner he can make passes over the region with his hands, saturating it with the electromagnetic energy flowing from his fingers and speak to it mentally, not violently, but firmly and tell it just what he wants it to do. The electromagnetic energy will convey his commands to the group or organ.

If, for example, the liver is sluggish, he will talk to it and tell it to become more active. If the heart is too active, he will talk to it firmly and ask it to slow down. He can tell the stomach to take care in handling foods. But before giving any command he will be certain that the action he requests will actually assist in restoring health. So it is that his training and years of experience will stand him in good stead. His diagnosis, like that of a qualified medical practitioner, is generally correct.

If, during the treatment, the electromagnetic energy does not flow abundantly from the Wirinun's hands into the patient, he will rub them briskly together, clenching and unclenching them rapidly, shake them vigorously and ensure that there is a great circulation of blood in his hands which will carry the electromagnetic energy into the patient's body.

Treatments are given in various positions. For example, when the spine needs attention the patient lies face downwards so that the hands can be moved down along the spine, with one hand on either side of the vertebral column. When it is necessary to direct the energies into the front part of the body, the patient lies on his or her back. An important factor is that whatever the treatment, the spine should be kept fairly straight and free from bend and strains so as not to hamper the flow of the electromagnetic energy.

The Wirinun realises that surgery must be used in some instances to save life and does actually recommend it in certain cases. He does appreciate the various remedies, massage, chiropractic and other types of treatment which often yield excellent results and he offers his healing technique as another method of preserving health. Even though his methods have been scoffed at by many white people, I cannot help but feel that this so-called "Bush Medicineman" has a technique which we could well learn to use.

It is a treatment that has been used successfully for centuries amongst the Aboriginal people and while the

Wirinun does not have a university diploma to say that he has mastered his studies, he is revered and respected amongst his people because of results he obtains.

Thousands of case histories prove that this healing technique bears further investigation.

AFTERWORD

Many elements of Aboriginal culture have been lost forever because of Europization. When HMS Supply dropped anchor at Sydney Cove on 26th January, 1788, it was the beginning of the end of tribal life as it had been for 50,000 years or more. The British settlers saw an unfamiliar and threatening environment and began changing it to satisfy their needs.

They imported new plants for cultivation and animals for domestication. They altered the environment by overstocking and introduced rabbits for sport. Destroyed natural plant life and hastened the extinction of many animal species. Within one hundred years the white settlers had overcome harsh and difficult conditions to establish the highest standard of living in the world on a per capita basis.

Aborigines were unable to survive the impact of Europization on their fragile culture and most faced tragic extinction. Six months after the arrival of the First Fleet settlers there was conflict between the two cultures. Nine months later, the Aboriginal population at Port Jackson began to die of smallpox, a disease introduced by white settlers. A second major Aboriginal smallpox epidemic occurred again in the 1820's.

Reflecting on historical evidence of more than two hundred years, their eventual integration into a white society seems inevitable. There are too few full blood, initiated Elders left to ensure the survival of a culture that has everywhere been influenced by white Australian society and its values.

Today's reality is not a product of Aboriginal culture. Too much has changed for either cultures to go back in time to revive the old ways. In some tribes no one is alive with sufficient knowledge and authority to be responsible for the perpetuation of ancient laws and rituals. Those who were adept at rainmaking and other magical practices are now dead. Few are interested in their history, rituals and customs. Their once intricate hunting methods with the use of spears and nulla nullas have been replaced with rifles.

Of the two hundred languages spoken by Aborigines in 1788 and as complex as Latin and Greek, there are now less than one hundred of those languages left and these are only spoken by a few people. Ten languages are spoken by the majority of Aborigines and it is believed that at least eight of these languages will become extinct by the end of this century.

Even in remote areas of the continent there is a disintegration of family life. As in white society, the children are left to their own devices and become law-breakers, their parents are suffering from alcohol abuse and betrayal by their own leaders. Many will not accept personal responsibility for their own actions. Both urban and outback Aborigines suffer chronic health problems, such as diabetes, heart disease, obesity, hypertension and sexually transmitted diseases.

As they become more Westernised they embrace the constraints of modern Western cultural values and by so doing, lose their inner freedom, identity and magical powers. Like most Westerners, they too are conditioned and manipulated into believing that money buys freedom, respect and self-esteem. Mining and technology has violated the landscape and the rivers changing the psychic vibrations of the Australian continent to such a degree that the traditional lifestyle of the indigenous Australian is disappearing. Those who have the courage to reject Western culture with its materialistic enticements and return to the ancient lifestyle, philosophy, law and language will regain their spirit and life and connect with their own inner essence.

Aborigines legally control more than one-eighth of Australia's surface, most of their land is in the Northern Territory. There are around 170,000 Aborigines living in Australia of which only a few are full blood initiates. This contrasts with the varied opinion which place the total Aboriginal population in 1788 between 300,000 and 1.5 million.

Those who choose to live a traditional lifestyle should be allowed to do so without social welfare payments and unemployment benefits. Government policy and administration has failed to solve the two hundred year old collision of cultures.

Cheque-book benevolence and the spending of millions of dollars a year by governments, will not exorcise a national guilt which some white Australian's may feel because of mistakes made by white ancestors. Hand-outs are patronising and smother initiative and do nothing to enhance the dignity and nobility that was once the birthright of the black Australian.

Spiritual and cultural roots cannot be restored by black militancy or million dollar hand-outs in mining royalties. Nor will the handing back of great tracts of land renew the Dreaming. It is more likely to create, in time, an apartheid situation or one of separate sovereignty.

There is no reason why the few remaining full blood, traditionalists should not be left to live on a separate black tribal area, commensurate with their numbers, free from interference by Government bureaucracy and the influences, good and bad, of a white society. Only under such conditions would they be able to maintain their own group identity. Whites controlling Aboriginal communities is detrimental to the revival of Aboriginal culture, if such a process is possible, considering the sad fact of so many traditions being lost forever.

Aboriginal people who choose to live in the established Australian society ought to be given assistance and the encouragement to do so; this means full citizenship of the Australian Commonwealth, with all its rights, privileges, responsibilities and duties.

The evidence available suggests that ~ like the culture of the ancient Egyptians ~ all that will remain will be various sites, artefacts, rock and decorative art, myths, legends and written history to remind future generations that a rich, unique and complex cultural tradition once existed on the Australian continent.

~Yvonne Malykke

Glossary

Alcheringa: Dreamtime. The beginning of creation.

Bahloo: The Moon.

Baiame: God the Creator. The all-pervading Supreme Intelligence. The first spiritual substance from which matter is composed and projected into manifestation.

Bora: Sacred ritual.

Bora Ring: Sacred initiation grounds. Sacred circle.

Bullima: World of the spirits.

Bunbulama: Rainmaking spirit.

Corroboree: Ritual and ceremony of a religious nature.

Dowie: A subtle dimension of existence usually following death and known as the next life. Similar to the astral world of psychic science. The Dowie dimension can only be experienced in a Dowie body. It also contains the memory bank.

Dreamtime: A dimension of being where the spirit ancestors reside and where the permanent records of the history of generations of the Australian Aboriginal people are kept. These are illustrated in pictographs, rock and bark paintings, ceremonies and oral teachings.

Gayandi: A Bullroarer comprised of a flat, oval-shaped piece of wood suspended from a string at one end. It is highly magnetised and contains the spirit of the Bora and is regarded as a sacred object.

Kungullun: Thoughts. The most powerful of all forces to influence our lives.

Marrgon: Ancestral spirit of thunder and lightning.

Marmoo: The spirit of evil from the lower realms of the Dowie.

Mimi: Rock spirits or elementals. Elongated in appearance.

Mullee Mullee: Dream spirits.

Mullowill: Etheric or subtle sheath surrounding the physical form and Dowie of all living things. Electro-magnetic body.

Narmingatha: Prayers directed to Baiame, Dreamtime ancestors and Totemic ancestors.

Nungeena: Mother Nature, spirit of the Dreamtime.

Punjel: Architect of the Universe, spirit of the Dreamtime.

Thalaualla: The black snake. Totem of the Warramunga Tribe.

Tintookies: Elemental spirits who inhabit the bush.

Tintuppa: Elemental spirits of the plants.

Tjuringa: Carved or painted pieces of wood or stone associated with the spirit world and regarded as sacred.

Totem: A class of material objects regarded with superstitious respect. It is believed that there exists an intimate relationship between the Aborigine and the object. The totem may be an ancestor of the tribe or individual which has taken the form of an animal or plant. Totemic laws are the constitution of Aboriginal life.

Tumpinyeri Mooroop: The Life Spirit of Electromagnetic energy.

Tya: Earth.

Uluru: Rainbow Serpent.

Wandjina: Creative spirits. Elementals of Earth, Water, Fire, Air and Seasons.

Walkabout: Going to the Bora ground for a special ritual for the Totem or for some other purpose such as the Shaman contacting the spirit world for rain. The initiate has to go to the Bora ground every year to practise certain ritualistic disciplines to improve character and to receive knowledge from the Elders. The young initiate works his way up by degrees and as ritual knowledge increases so does his status in the tribe.

Wirinun: Shaman, Medicineman, Wiseman, Magician.

Wirlies: Bark shelters made of a basic frame of tree branches to which are attached long strips of bark.

Wuluwaid: Rainmaking spirit.

Yhi: Sun goddess, spirit of the Dreamtime.

Yowie: Soul. A subtle essence that incarnates in human form and has evolved from innumerable lower forms of life.

OTHER COSMOS BOOKS

MEMORIES AND REFLECTIONS OF A PIONEER
AUSTRALIA 1875 - 1939
by Denis O'Callaghan

Denis O'Callaghan was one of the earliest of the pioneers who followed Bayley and Ford into Coolgardie after the discovery of that El Dorado in August, 1892. He experienced all the varied emotions of those hectic times, the heat and mirage, the dust and flies, the fever and dysentery, the nights of revelry in the Denver City and other Bayley Street hotels, the sly-grog shops and the two-up and Murrumbidgee rings.

With his mates, he shared the sparse food and water supplies, pelted helter-skelter to this reported "rush" and that, and came back, more often than not, tired, disappointed and broke only to spring, re-awakened, to another sortie where the prospectors' "nugget-kickers" led out into the shimmering and pitiless Never Never.

Dinny has passed along to posterity a valuable addition to early Australian goldfields history, which is greatly to his credit, adding to the sum total of the all too little recorded past of the glamorous, golden days of pioneering Australia.

Those who were not so fortunate as to have shared in the halcyon days of Coolgardie and the Back-O-Beyond, Dinny's memoirs will be read with keen enjoyment and the reader will depart from the last page with a sigh of regret that they, too, were not spectators of the scenes he has depicted, that they too did not share the mateships and the hardships that tested men out and tempered them as steel.

~Victor G.C. Riseley

In Pursuit of the Spiritual Cosmos

Yvonne Malykke

An overview of the New Age counter-culture revolution. An exciting and adventurous encounter with many well-known people who were instrumental in laying the foundation for this movement during the 1970's to the 90's. Informative and unique in its presentation and a useful guide to seekers on their spiritual journey. It is controversial, truthful, shocking, tragic, sensitive, sacred, mystical and philosophical.

What the Reviewers say:

"I loved it. I could not put it down. I read it in 24 hours non-stop. It was a very different kind of book then I have ever read before. It seemed to draw so many different elements together so that I could get a real overview of how spirituality, as a movement in this country has developed . . . It is a wonderful book. I can recommend it to anyone who is interested in spirituality and understanding themselves."

Ray Sheridan: Soul Safari 2SER-FM

"For those looking for some factual information on the early days of the whole New Age movement in Australia, or, a good read about this pioneering woman's important work in opening the consciousness to the diverse spiritual approaches available today, this book is a must." Leo Drioli, Editor Golden Age magazine

"I consider this book to be an interesting and enlightening piece of intellectual and social history."

Consciousness Magazine (Australian TransPersonal Assoc.)

". . . of interest to all people exploring new ways of living and seeing the world . . . A thoroughly fascinating book and an important contribution to the history of New Age concepts." New Dawn Magazine

254 pages: 28 b/w plates: $25.00: ISBN 09588588 5 3
Available from Cosmos Periodicals
PO Box 626 Murwillumbah, NSW Australia 2484